"*Awakened Relating* is an inspiring and thoro⬚ relationship as a way of embodying our awak⬚ wisdom as well as practical guidance about how ⬚o bring spiritual illumination into the very heart of our humanness. Highly recommended!"

> —**John Welwood**, author of *Perfect Love, Imperfect Relationships* and *Journey of the Heart*

"This is a wonderful and clear excursion into the inner life of intimacy. Lynn Marie leads us into our true Self, where love is already and always fully alive and ready to be shared. I found her insights profound and immensely comforting."

> —**David Richo**, author of *How to Be an Adult in Relationships*

"*Awakened Relating* dispels the myth of romantic love and points directly to an awakened way of relating that arises from the recognition of our true nature as Love. Clearly written, deeply insightful, and filled with illuminating interviews and powerful meditative inquiries, this book is a liberating guide to meet the most challenging areas of relationship from the light of Awareness. I highly recommend it!"

> —**John J. Prendergast, PhD**, author of *In Touch*

"Lynn Marie Lumiere brings together a clear understanding of initial awakening, psychotherapy, and intimate relationships in this cutting-edge book. Awakening has historically been practiced in monastic settings or as a solo journey. Today awakening is happening in the midst of our everyday lives. So, it is most important to bring openhearted awareness to our intimate relating. *Awakened Relating* is both an important and timely book that opens the dialogue about awakening and relationships."

> —**Loch Kelly**, author of *Shift into Freedom*

"Breaking new ground, this wise and eloquent book offers detailed guidance in embodying our radiant, boundless, undivided true nature in the realm of intimate relationships, where relational wounding and unresolved childhood issues may make it challenging to live from the limitless love we know ourselves to be."

> —**Stephan Bodian**, author of *Wake Up Now* and *Beyond Mindfulness*

"*Awakened Relating* is based on over forty years of daily, unrelenting commitment by Lynn Marie Lumiere to discover and share the egoless state of non-dual awareness in the midst of intimate relationships, and as a therapist of the highest caliber…. Lynn Marie's book is perhaps the first to show us, step by step, how couples living in this new millennium can support each other and realize their true non-dual nature in the ultimate wisdom of undivided, invincible love. This book is a watershed in the evolution of contemporary non-dual wisdom."

—**Peter Fenner, PhD**, author of the *Radiant Mind* and
Natural Awakening books and courses

"Using the context of intimate relationship, Lynn Marie invites us to a deep exploration of who we are and how this embodies moment by moment. I love the honesty and vulnerability in which she explores this highly relevant topic. This inquiry and its unfolding is at the cutting edge of spirituality and our human experience. In my view, awakened relating is a necessary step in our evolution that has relevance as to whether or not we survive as a species."

—**Isaac Shapiro**, non-dual teacher, and author of
It Happens by Itself

"With clarity, humility, and wisdom, Lynn Marie Lumiere invites the reader into a deep exploration of the undivided and loving Awareness that is at once the source of life and the ultimate healing of our conditioned separation and suffering. The author's devotion to truth shines through each page as she offers examples from her own life's journey, her work as a psychotherapist, and meditative inquiries, as well as interviews with individuals and couples who seem to be embodying 'awakened relating.' In pointing to that which dissolves separation and has the greatest power to transform our lives, Lynn Marie invites us back home to the Love inherent in our *being*."

—**Dorothy Hunt**, author of *Only This!* and
Leaves from Moon Mountain

"*Awakened Relating* is a beautifully written, thought-provoking book that sheds light on the myriad ways the discovery of the undivided nature of reality can so radically alter the landscape of our relationships. Through examples from her own relationship and compelling interviews with both clients and teachers she has worked with, Lynn Marie explores how the recognition that we *are* the very fulfillment, wholeness, and love we've historically sought in our relationships frees us up to love more harmoniously, more unreservedly, more openly, and more fearlessly."

—**John Astin, PhD**, author of *Searching for Rain in a Monsoon*

"*Awakened Relating* reveals a new direction for our looking, where we discover love that is already present, that pervades everywhere, that is independent of another, that is available no matter how we're feeling about our partner, and that is independent of our life circumstances.... Lumiere beautifully points out the one true undivided love that is everlasting, can be interwoven into all our human relationships, contains all the happiness we could ever want, and is delivered fresh each moment of our lives. *Awakened Relating* is accessible, powerful, and enlightening to read. I couldn't put this book down and will be recommending it to all my friends and colleagues."

—**Richard Miller, PhD**, author of *The iRest Program for Healing PTSD*

"In this inspiring book, Lynn Marie has systematically revealed her deep understanding of the myths and realities of love relationships. She has synthesized two vast topics—love relationships and non-duality—and provided a map for embodying unconditional openness as a fully lived, real experience in the midst of the challenges of intimate relationships. The book is peppered with her own revelations, as well as juicy interviews and stories of clients and teachers who are awakening from the dream of relationships to the reality of what awakened relating offers. The exercises she offers at the end of each chapter are easy to do, practical, and inspiring. I love this book!"

—**Penny Fenner**, coauthor of *Essential Wisdom Teachings*

"*Awakened Relating* is an important milestone in the maturing field integrating non-dual wisdom with Western psychology. This book takes the conversation regarding relationship as a path to awakening a step further. Offering a generous helping of illustrative examples, Lynn Marie Lumiere points out how discovering and relaxing into unconditioned presence is the golden key unlocking non-defensive intimacy, relational harmony, and wholehearted sexual delight.... I sincerely recommend this book to those who understand, or have had a glimpse, or even just an inkling (as Lynn Marie suggests), that in order to awaken *out* of a conditioned relating, one must awaken *to* unconditioned relating. This book points the way."

—**Ken Bradford, PhD**, author of *The I of the Other*

"Just reading *Awakened Relating* opened an access to relational awakening for me that is openhearted, intellectually clear, and meaningful. Whether we are looking for love to come to us, in a loving relationship, or contemplating exploring the perfect union, reading *Awakened Relating* will allow us to see who and what we really are—even if this is only for a short moment, and then another, and then another. As a non-dual psychotherapist, I especially enjoyed Lynn Marie's interviews with people from all walks of life, and her appreciation of the wisdom of both our conditioned self and our undivided Self. Every couple and individual will benefit from reading this, whether they are 'beginners' or 'old-timers' to the awakening process. Thank you for writing this!"

—**Judith Orloff**, author of *Choices for Success*

awakened relating

A GUIDE TO EMBODYING

UNDIVIDED LOVE IN

INTIMATE RELATIONSHIPS

LYNN MARIE LUMIERE, MFT

New Harbinger Publications, Inc.

Publisher's Note

Distributed in Canada by Raincoast Books

Copyright © 2018 by Lynn Marie Lumiere
        Non-Duality Press
        An imprint of New Harbinger Publications, Inc.
        5674 Shattuck Avenue
        Oakland, CA 94609
        www.newharbinger.com

"Gazing into Oneness Together," in chapter 11, is adapted with permission from the work of Sperry Andrews, founder/co-director at the Human Connection Institute: http://www.connectioninstitute.org.

"Meditation on Moving from Stillness," in chapter 9, is adapted with permission from the work of Lyn Hunstad, http://www.TempleOfAuthenticDivinity .com.

Cover design by Amy Shoup

Acquired by Ryan Buresh

Edited by Erin Raber

All Rights Reserved

Library of Congress Cataloging-in-Publication Data on file

20   19   18

10   9   8   7   6   5   4   3   2   1   First Printing

This is dedicated to the One I love,

and to my beloved John, a loving expression of the One.

May this book be of benefit.

Contents

Preface: An Evolutionary Imperative   vii

Introduction   1

PART I: Awakening Undivided Love

1   Waking Up from the Dream of Separation:
Awakened Relating   13

2   The Most Important Thing: Awakening to the
Source of Love   27

3   The Accepting Heart: Awakening Self-Love   43

4   The Madness of the Gods: Falling in Love   55

PART II: Awakened Relating in Practice

5   The Challenged Heart: Relational Wounding   67

6   Mending the Wounded Heart: Healing With
Awakened Relating   79

7   The Undivided Heart: Awakened Conflict
Resolution   93

8   Telling It Like It Is: Awakened Communication   109

9   One Love, Two Bodies: Awakened Sexuality   121

PART III: Living Undivided Love Together

10   Living Love: Staying Awake Together   139

11   A Love That Knows No Other: True Intimacy   153

12   Love in Action: Changing Our World Through
     Awakened Relating   171

     Appendix: Additional Stories of Awakened Relating   187

     Acknowledgments   197

     References   199

Preface
An Evolutionary Imperative

I have come to believe that the next evolutionary step for our species in these challenging times is to discover a new way of relating that is rooted in what is true—that we all come from the same source. We all share the same essential nature. As more of us recognize this and begin to relate to each other from this most essential truth, it will bring more justice, equality, sanity, Love, compassion, and kindness into our world. This applies to intimate relationships, which are the focus of this book, but also to all the ways we relate to others. It is time to forsake the old ways of relating based on the illusion of separation and step into this new frontier of learning to relate from the truth of our shared Being.

We are all being called to evolve more quickly than ever before. The survival of the Earth herself is now threatened. As individuals and as a species, we need to recognize that we all exist within one unified field of Love that permeates all life. We won't survive for long if we continue to ignore how we are shredding the ecological and social fabric of interconnectedness that sustains life on this planet. We are called to awaken to the truth that we do not exist separately from each other or from our environment. When we believe we are separate, life does not flow, and our relationships lack harmony and true connection. Over time, this has led to increasing amounts of inequality, greed, violence, and injustice.

Many of today's spiritual leaders are giving us strong warnings. Barbara Marx Hubbard (2006) states, "We are now living through an evolutionary crisis. If we, as a culture, continue to function in the same way, we will see the demise of our life support system itself. This is a huge wake up call."

In the same vein, Eckhart Tolle (2005) warns that, "Humanity is now faced with a stark choice: Evolve or die.... If the structures of the human mind remain unchanged, we will always end up recreating the same world, the same evils, the same dysfunction."

Adyashanti (2012) states, "We are no doubt at a very critical point in time. Our world hangs in the balance, and a precarious balance it is. Awakening to reality is no longer a possibility; it is an imperative. ... Wake up or perish is the spiritual call of our times. Could we ever need more motivation than this?"

Paradoxically, it is equally true to say on the most fundamental level that *all is well* with the world, just as it is. Our challenge is to recognize this, while also seeing the necessity of evolving our consciousness and awakening together. Because of this necessity, the planetary consciousness is shifting to allow awakening to our true nature to be known by a larger percentage of the population than ever before. Access to teachers and teachings that can direct us to awakening are now available to everyone who is open to receiving them. The only requirement is an open heart.

Introduction

We all long to find everlasting love in our intimate, primary relationships. Yet, for many of us, these relationships are often fraught with frustration and pain. Have you ever wondered why romance starts out with so much passion and promise and then tends to fizzle before ending in disappointment or conflict?

What will it take to finally experience the lasting love that you have always longed for? Is it even possible to know a love that does not come and go? How can we experience an ever-present love in intimate relationship? These are questions that I asked myself for many years. Somehow, I could not settle for love that was temporary, inconsistent, and conditional. I longed for a deeper love, one that was not limited to human relationships, but could be experienced within them. The longing to experience a true love within myself and in close relationships is what propelled me to the discovery I am sharing with you in this book.

I discovered that relating within the truth of our shared Being radically changes the way we are in life and in relationships. Romantic relationships in particular have become burdened with demands to produce lasting love and happiness. I will be showing how it is possible to know an Undivided Love that does not come and go, and how to share that in our lives and in our intimate partnerships. We will be exploring how knowing this everlasting Love has the potential to heal and resolve the issues we face in relationships at their root.

My Journey into Undivided Love

This book was borne out of my own experience of awakening and healing, as well as my awareness of the great need for relationships to be more aligned with the deepest truth of life. The pain of not being able to satisfy my deepest longing in romantic love ignited my journey toward the source of Love. It took repeated failures before I could finally let go of my fierce attachment to the deeply held impulse to reach for love in others. I wanted the love that I believed could be provided only by another human being, not just a mysterious, intangible Love within. I did not yet realize that the way to fully experience love with another human being is to find the infinite source of Love within myself. Only then is it possible to release our attachment to getting love from others, and we can share it with everyone.

The great wisdom teachings of all traditions tell us that we all share a deeper, divine nature that includes our human nature. I became committed to knowing my true nature first-hand, through direct experience. Nothing seemed more important to me than realizing this truth. I sensed that tapping into an infinite source of Love would spare me the endless frustrations and suffering I experienced in searching for love in people, places, and things that were, at best, inconsistent reflections of real love. I was also searching for a way to heal my relational wounding from childhood. I came to realize that what was needed was *both* a realization of my essential nature and the ability to bring that loving presence to my wounding. Focusing on either one alone proved incomplete.

My spiritual search has spanned my entire adult life and has involved many traditions, such as Christianity, Buddhism, Hinduism, as well as paths outside of traditions. My involvement with nondual wisdom teachings (based on the belief that the totality of all life and all experience is interconnected) began in 1992. I discovered Western spiritual teachers who could speak nondual truth in a vernacular that was familiar and understandable. I was deeply drawn to these teachings. For almost two decades, my root teacher has been Adyashanti, although many teachers of nonduality, as well as Tibetan Buddhist Dzogchen, have influenced me. These influences are woven throughout this book.

I am aware that these nondual wisdom teachings are not the only ways to tap into the truth of who we are. We each have our own unique path. Since 1998, I have also been involved with the exploration of nondual wisdom and psychotherapy, a new wave in psychology that blends nondual realization and therapeutic skills to resolve our psychological and emotional imbalances.

In my work as a Marriage and Family Therapist, I help my clients apply nondual wisdom to their relationship issues. No matter what the presenting issue is, therapy always seems to include working on the relationship with our self and with others. I was deeply interested in finding the root cause of the struggles I was experiencing and witnessing. There are many solutions being offered to solve relationship problems today, yet in my experience, none of them get to the source of the problem. To truly solve any problem, we must trace it to its source. I see the belief that we are separate from Undivided Love and each other as the *root* cause of relational turmoil and human suffering. All solutions that point elsewhere can only hope to offer temporary or partial relief. Through my experience, I have found that a connection to a deeper source of wisdom, Love, and unity needs to be included in order to truly resolve our relational disharmony. Our limited, conditioned mind is not an independent source of power that can provide true transformation of our painful, habitual patterns.

About the Book

Awakened Relating was written for all of us who share a longing to know an ever-present Love and to experience that deeply within our self and with our intimate partners. It is for everyone, whether you are in an intimate partnership or not. This book is for anyone who is interested in awakening to the truth of who they are and exploring how human relationships can work better and be more fulfilling. It is also for those of us who want to bring a more evolved relating to our global community in order to create more peace in our divided world. There is an opportunity for greater unity in all relating when we stop focusing on our differences and come to see that we are all part of one inclusive whole.

I called upon many other voices to join me in this exploration of embodying this pinnacle wisdom in intimate relationships. My intention is to start a global conversation about how we can all be more awake in our relating. I felt that my voice alone would have limited the range that I wanted to offer and explore. I conversed with people from seven different countries for this book. Some are spiritual teachers, some are friends or members of my spiritual community, and some are my psychotherapy clients. Even though their circumstances and backgrounds vary, their stories and mine all illustrate how what I term "awakened relating" is now becoming a lived reality for many people. I use pseudonyms for some of the people sharing conversations and stories. Those who were willing to share their full names and contact information are listed on my website at http://www.lynnmarielumiere .com.

Chapters

Each chapter discusses awakened relating as it applies to different aspects of relationship, such as falling in love, the challenge of relational wounding, self-love, dealing with conflict, communication, sexuality, and intimacy. In each chapter, under the heading "Practicing Awakened Relating," you'll find a story or a conversation that demonstrates how individuals and couples are experiencing awakened relating in their lives. Other examples of this are also peppered throughout the chapters. There are additional complete stories and conversations in the Appendix. The stories and conversations show that awakened relating can, and is, happening for ordinary people, not just spiritual teachers.

Each chapter ends with a "Meditative Inquiry" that offers an opportunity for you to reflect on what's being shared and to experience it directly. I invite you to spend time with the Meditative Inquiries. It is an experiential, rather than a conceptual, understanding of the deepest truth that frees us. Therefore, it is highly beneficial to be open to receiving the direct experience that the Meditative Inquiries offer. I recommend using a journal to write about your experience with each exercise. This is a good way to deepen and clarify your understanding. I suggest you especially spend some time with Chapter 2, which elaborates ways to recognize and embody the Undivided Love that is our nature.

Key Terms

Some of the terms that are central to this book may not be familiar to everyone. We are all at different points of our individual paths to Love and wholeness. As follows, I offer brief definitions to several key terms to aid you on your journey through this book. You may want to refer back to this section as our use of these terms grows and develops.

Awakening

There are many ideas and concepts about what spiritual awakening is. Some people believe that you are either awake or unawake in an all or nothing way. You may believe that awakening is something that just comes out of nowhere by grace and, *boom*, you are now forever awake to the truth of who you are. Although that can happen, it is very rare, and even then, the full embodiment of such a shift takes time. For most of us, awakening is a gradual unfolding over time that begins with our first glimpse of our true nature and is the result of a combination of grace and great dedication.

In this book, I am primarily focusing on the first step of awakening, which is recognizing the ever-present awareness that is aware of reading this page and everything else in your environment. You can simply see that you are aware. Becoming "aware of being aware" is the first step. From here, we have the opportunity to return to this noticing again and again, allowing its presence to grow more evident and become embodied in our relationships and our life. One of my main intentions with this book is to take awakening out of the seemingly unreachable distant heavens and bring it down to its immediate availability here and now.

Awakened Relating

Awakened relating springs from the process of awakening itself. As our awakening matures, it is revealed that we are not separate from each other and our world. Awakened relating means that we relate to others with this understanding. The practice of this understanding in our relationships awakens our heart and opens new dimensions of inti-macy including awakened sexuality and awakened communication. Awakened relating teaches us to rely on our deeper nature, allowing the essence of our shared Being to be a loving, compassionate presence in relationship that is capable of resolving all interpersonal issues in its infinite wisdom. There are times when all of us, even the most enlight-ened, fall back on duality in our intimate relationships. Yet, awakened relating can increasingly occur in the unfolding of our infinite awakening.

I prefer to use the word "relating" because it refers to an ongoing, living dynamic within one interconnected whole. The word relation-ship connotes a static "thing" experienced between two people. Also, I want to note that we can have a conscious relationship and still be relating within a divided, dualistic framework as two separate entities. Awakened relating includes conscious relationship, but within the larger context of Undivided Love.

Nonduality

Nonduality refers to the fact that the totality of all life and all experience is one interconnected whole. We have been conditioned to perceive this wholeness as divided up into self and other and self and world as if they were, in fact, separate, and not interdependent and inextricably connected. Dividing love with our dualistic minds has resulted in losing contact with the one Undivided Love that unites us all.

Nondual truth is perceived as paradoxical by the dualistic mind because practically everything one could say about it, the opposite can be said too. Essentially, the nondual view does not see exclusively in either/or terms, such as right or wrong or true or false. Within this understanding, the polarized dualities of our conditioned mind are included in a larger frame. It is challenging to speak of nonduality with dualistic language. In fact, the nondual truth can never be fully stated in words. As Adyashanti states in chapter 12, "The truth is the one thing that can't be stated." It can only be pointed to.

I am not speaking to your dualistic, conditioned mind in this book. I am speaking to your true nature, the essence of your Being, which already knows the truth, even if your conscious mind still does not.

True Nature

Our true nature is the deepest, most essential truth of who we are beyond all the thoughts, beliefs, concepts, feelings, and sensations that make up our known identity. This is what we are awakening to. It is a mystery, and it is the Undivided Love that we experience in the process of awakened relating. I use many terms for this ineffable, true nature that are all synonymous: essential nature, basic nature, awareness, presence, true Self, Being, essence, Love, reality, the unconditioned, and natural state. Using many terms helps the mind to not fixate on any particular term, which can then become a reified concept, rather than a living experience. There are no words that can adequately describe the indescribable. Ultimately, our true nature is beyond labels and descriptions entirely. Although we must use language to point to what is unnamable, the living essence of our Being cannot be captured in words.

Separate Self

The separate self is nothing more than a collection of thoughts, feelings, sensations, and perceptions that co-arise with the world we experience. All this arises within the vast field of awareness that is our essential identity. The apparent separate self is not a separate entity that exists independent of this field of awareness. Yet, we become identified with our thinking, feeling, and sensing, which creates a mentally constructed sense of self in relation to a mentally constructed separate other, as well as a world separate from our self. In addition to the term separate self, I use terms such as conditioned identity, egoic identity, ego, ego-self, divided self, and separate identity. They all point to the same imagined identity that we have come to perceive as our individual, personal self that exists separately from others and all life.

Undivided Love

We are all very familiar with divided love, which is relating from the belief in separation from others and Love's source. The most popular version of divided love is the story of romance, which involves finding "the one" who will provide us with everlasting love and happiness. The Undivided Love I am referring to here is the energy, or conscious life force, that permeates all of existence. This life force can be called Love because it is all-inclusive and unconditionally allowing of everything *as it is*. It is a quiet benevolence that emanates pure compassion. This truest Love is undivided in that it is not separate from anything or anyone, and is therefore fully intimate with all that is. It is the one unifying field subsuming all of creation. As this Love becomes directly known and experienced, an openhearted, radiant Love for everything and everyone opens up inside us, illuminating how we relate. As we come to know our true nature, we discover that Love is its very essence.

I capitalize the word Love to distinguish this absolute, infinite Love and quality of our true nature from other forms of love, such as romantic or human love. I also capitalize Undivided Love, Being, and Self to distinguish them from the same words when they are not used to designate an absolute reality.

How to Get the Most Benefit From this Book

Whether you see yourself as awake or unawake, you may find value in the pointers that I offer throughout this book for both awakening and its embodiment, specifically in intimate relationships. Whether nonduality is a new subject to you or you already have a deep understanding of nondual wisdom, what's most important is that you are where you are now. You can only move from where you actually are, and then trust the understanding to reveal your next steps in this magnificent unfolding.

It is most helpful to relax your mind and open your heart to allow a *felt-sense* of what is being read to emerge. Be aware of the initially subtle nuances of feeling and perception that the words begin to evoke within you. To the best of your ability, allow your experience of this book to be a contemplation or a meditation, rather than an intellectual study. I believe you'll get the most benefit this way. For me, writing this book was a meditation. The truth conveyed here cannot be expressed or understood with the intellect alone.

Although you may be searching for a solution to your relationship problems, the more you can allow yourself to relax, the more likely you will find it here. As you relax into openness, a sense of what is being communicated will arise within your heart and body, which can then illuminate the mind. If the mind gets too busily involved and confusion arises, relax, let go, and open your heart again. This is how you can best receive what is being offered here.

Happily Ever After

In my experience, the "happily ever after" that we all seek in romantic relationships is found not through "the one" right person of romantic novels and films, but through the one, capital-L Love that will never leave us, no matter what is happening in our relationships. Taking the presence of this Love into intimate relating is an ongoing journey of discovery and wonder that leads to ever-increasing amounts of shared Love and joy. I now know that no person can provide all that my heart longs for; only the deepest truth of who I am is capable of that. Not only is the Love we seek always available, our essential nature *is* that Love.

I am excited to share this understanding with you and invite you to discover a whole new way of relating that will reveal the infinite source of Love and happiness that can never leave you. It is time to let go of the fairy tale and embrace true intimacy through *Awakened Relating!*

PART I

Awakening
Undivided Love

CHAPTER 1

Waking Up from the Dream of Separation
Awakened Relating

The dream of love distracts us from finding
The love that is ever present.

—John Welwood

When we see with the eyes of Undivided Love, we recognize the beauty in all existence. We see the sacred that lies in the heart of all beings. We see the world with new eyes, free of the filters of the conditioned mind that divides the world up into so many polarities, such as us and them, you and me, good and bad, or right and wrong. True Love is undivided. It sees and delights in all of its magnificent displays equally. It does not see anything as separate from itself. Through the eyes of Love, we see everyone as our other Self in a full embrace of complete acceptance. From the vantage point of Love and clarity, nothing needs to change; yet all that appears to be out of alignment with Love naturally moves toward balance and harmony.

Most of humanity has fallen asleep to this truth and does not see through the eyes of true Love. Many are still longing to wake up from the dream of separation with the kiss of romantic love. It is commonly believed that romantic relationships will free us from the deep sense of fear, lack, and insecurity that is inherent in the belief that we are each separate entities. Yet, many people are taking notice of the fact that conventional relationships based in a divided love are not fulfilling their promise. This motivates us to look for a deeper solution that ultimately leads to the discovery of an Undivided Love, which unites us all.

When we bring that discovery to our intimate relating, it is "awakened relating." In awakened relating, we enjoy the unique expression of both our Self and the other without losing the experience of our shared unity. This is living an awakened understanding in our relating. Or, if we do not yet have this understanding, we can come to it through practicing awakened relating. We can practice it with whatever understanding we do have.

Awakened relating is relying on whatever sense we have of our deeper nature and allowing its infinite wisdom to resolve all relationship issues. This is the deepest of all solutions because it goes to the root of all problems—the sense of a divided self that arises from being out of touch with our undivided nature. When we pull weeds out by the top, they appear to be gone temporarily, but they grow back. When we pull them out by the root, they don't grow back. If there's no belief in a separate self, there are no problems. There are situations that may need attention, but the perception of a problem comes from the fear-based, imaginary separate self. Solutions to relationship problems that are created out of a dualistic consciousness are often temporary, and the problem arises again, possibly in another form. It can go on endlessly. We don't need to solve every single problem that arises in relationship; we just need to find the one solution that resolves them all. This book is about resolving relationship problems at the root.

The Dream of Separation

The first step in waking from a dream is to realize that we have been dreaming. When we wake up in the morning, the seeming reality of a dream vanishes as soon as we realize it was only a dream. If we believe the deeply imprinted fantasies about relationship to be true, we will hold onto them. As I learned from my own experience, we will not let go of reaching for love outside ourselves until it is quite clear that it is not found there. As we become more consciously aware that the fantasy does not deliver on its promises, we can let it go. Let us inquire into the dream of separation.

The imprint of separation starts with our transition from the womb into this world; we leave the oceanic feeling of oneness with our mother and begin our journey as a separate individual. This is reinforced daily by the appearance of separate objects, which we learn to name and describe. The baby learns to name his or her body and other bodies, as well as all objects, and begins to see them as separate, independent, and other. The perception and experience of separation is systematically reinforced throughout life in our families, schools, and religions.

We tend to regard everything we can name, including ourselves, as a separate "thing." Yet, life is one interrelated whole that expresses itself as diversity within unity. Everything that appears within our awareness and experience exists in and *as* an expression of the singular source. Every human, animal, and plant on Earth breathes some of the same molecules that have already been breathed by all other living beings. Nothing happens or appears independently of everything else. The trees cannot exist without the soil, sunshine, rain, and air. And, neither can we. Nothing exists in isolation.

Quantum physics has turned our ideas about matter, energy, and space upside down and suggests an underlying unity, while chaos theory suggests that a change in any one part of the whole affects everything in the universe. Einstein discovered that what we perceive as matter is really a lower vibration of the same one energy. Matter can appear to be a separate "thing," but it is not. What we perceive as physical reality is not "out there" and separate from us. Scientists have discovered the Observer Effect, which tells us that subatomic particles require an observing consciousness to form a reality. Unknowingly, we create every object in the world simply by giving attention to it. The way we look at objects or others determines what we see. Therefore, it is possible to consciously create our reality in line with our highest intentions for Love and harmony. Understanding this can radically change the way we are in relationship. This intellectual understanding of nonseparation, supported by science, can be a starting point for the journey from the experience of being separate into a deeper realization of the unity of all life and our creative potential.

The Divided Self

The divided self is a mind-made idea that is created by us in concert with the people around us when we are very little children. This is the way we are inducted into perceiving ourselves as a thing in relation to all other things, which is the basis for the illusion of separation within which we all have been living. This apparent divided self is only made of thoughts and the feelings, sensations, and perceptions associated with them, which never creates an actual entity. Our sense of "self" is not more than our current thoughts that continually change and pass by. Attached to these thoughts is the "I-thought," which gives us a sense of a "me" that is thinking the thoughts, and the separate self that the thoughts are about. The "I-thought" creates the idea that, "I am Lynn" (or John, Mary, Sam, etc.), "I am a body," "I am hungry," or "I am happy," and so on. When there is no "I-thought," there is no divided and separate self. It is important to see what remains when we let go of thoughts, even for a moment. As an infant, before any labeling and describing occurred, and before the "I-thought" arose, the background of awareness that is our true Self was always present. It was not born and it cannot die.

The divided self only exists as a belief in the mind and a felt sense in the body. Becoming free of the conditioned feeling of separation from others that lives in the body can be the most challenging. We may have a deep realization of our undivided nature and still *feel* a bodily sense of separation. We can use the power of our awareness to examine the separation we feel in the body and see that it is only ever-changing sensations floating in the field of awareness.

Searching for Love

It is common to think of the divided self as the ego. The ego is the mechanism by which we identify ourselves as separate. It is not an actual thing or self. The ego's underlying felt sense of disconnected-ness creates a chronic sense of lack and insecurity that we are always seeking relief from. The belief that we must get love from others is part of that chronic seeking, and is largely unconscious. Even if we know intellectually that this is not true, upon close examination, we may see that on a deeper, unconscious level, we do believe this. Even those who pursue spiritual awakening and have a genuine understanding may still find themselves acting as if Love is found in a separate other. This misunderstanding can be one of the greatest obstacles to finding true Love and then sharing it, not only with a special other, but with all beings. Adyashanti (1999) says:

> It is in the arena of personal relationship that the illusion of the separate self clings most tenaciously and insidiously. Indeed, there is nothing that derails more spiritual seekers than the grasping at and attaching to personal relationship. …Even with deep realization, people still continue to relate as though there is an "other." The identification with separation is incredibly strong. It is very, very deep, very strong.

Because of our identification with separation, we tend to seek ful-fillment outside our self in relationships, money, success, sex, material things, spirituality, and more. Until we recognize that what we are looking for is already within us, we will always seek something outside of us. The more we seek, the farther away we get from what is already here. This keeps us locked in the ego's sense of insecurity. It also keeps us feeling dependent and incomplete. We often believe that a relation-ship will eliminate these feelings and make us whole, but it cannot. As Zen teacher, Cheri Huber (1997) says, "Without a relationship I feel lacking, incomplete, inadequate, unfulfilled, and dissatisfied. I believe that when I am with someone things will be different; I will be happy, complete satisfied, etc. No, I won't." This does not work because it is a denial of the truth that we are already whole. Therefore, the satisfac-tion brought about through obtaining a new relationship is most often fleeting or inconsistent. The fact that we cannot be fully satisfied when denying our inherent wholeness is the compassionate wisdom of

infinite intelligence because it points us back to where Love and fulfillment are really found.

Wanting an intimate relationship is an integral part of our human
nature. The drive to connect and experience closeness is part of the
biological make-up of most mammals, including us. However, what I
am pointing to is even more fundamental than that. Our primordial
need, the one that is at the center of life itself, is the need to come into
conscious recognition of the truth of who we are, in the deepest sense.
Then, we can spontaneously and joyously share the Love we are with
our other Selves. Inside each one of us is a natural connection with
our shared Being. When allowed to, Undivided Love will express itself
in countless forms of awakened relating.

The primordial impulse to return home to our true nature is a
powerful force that can never be fulfilled through any relationship
alone. No relationship, no matter how good it may be, will ever fulfill
our need to know the Love that is our nature. As John Welwood says
in *Perfect Love, Imperfect Relationships* (2006), "No one else can ever
provide the connection that finally puts the soul at ease. We find that
connection when the window of the heart opens, allowing us to bask
in the warmth of our true nature."

Adyashanti (2006–2010) experienced this when he met his wife,
Mukti. He said, "I found the relationship of my dreams, and yet we
both knew, this isn't it, in and of itself. I saw it was not enough—that
even this isn't the end of this push inside. Nothing will take the place
of true freedom—nothing. It's just not going to happen."

A human being looking for Love is like a wave in the ocean
looking for water, believing it is separate from water. In essence, we *are*
the Love we seek. Although it is inherent and already present as our
own heart essence, it can be awakened in the presence of another. We
can share and enjoy Love with other human beings, but it just doesn't
come *from* them. Awakened relating is about sharing and celebrating
real Love together, rather than trying to get it from each other. Once
we know we are what we seek, it is possible to relate from a place of
freedom, harmony, and acceptance, rather than from lack, grasping,
and attachment. As we move into awakened relating, we enter the

timeless freedom that perfect Love offers. Awakened relating is the secret to lasting Love in relationship.

Carla: The Sacred Journey into Love's Source

Intimate relationship and sexuality have always been important doorways to a deeper knowing and presence for Carla. It was her first kiss as a teenager that introduced her to something she describes as, "uncontrived, spontaneous, natural, and pure" for the first time. She didn't know what that meant at the time, but it created a longing to know this experience more fully. Her interest in relationship and sexuality led Carla to be a body-oriented therapist, and a teacher of tantra, or sacred sexuality. The focus of her teaching is on the tantric art of transforming consciousness through accepting and allowing everything to be as it is.

The following is a conversation I had with Carla about her experience of discovering that Love is sourced within our Being, rather than from an imagined, separate other. I am touched by Carla's commitment to discovering true Love and by the depth of challenge she shares in coming to this understanding. It is a death of all that we have held true about intimate relationship, and a birth of a Love that is both unknown by the mind and intimately familiar to our heart essence. It is a sacred and courageous journey.

LML: The teaching that Love is found within is central to the tantra that you teach. Please share about that.

Carla: Yes, it is a central teaching in tantra that everything we look for is found inside ourselves, but this teaching is very easily misunderstood. Even though it sounds simple, it can be quite complicated, but it is extremely important to realize the truth of this teaching. For example, there are many different kinds of love. The first kind of love I discovered was the passionate kind of love—a love that is very full, sexual, overflowing, and joyous. There is also a sweet melting, merging love, where boundaries dissolve into an endless, timeless expanse. I have found these kinds of love in sex. Later as a therapist, I experienced a more compassionate love.

For me, it was important to be in relationship with another person in order to touch into these different types of love. However, I have also experienced the source of Love within on my own in meditation, particularly tantric meditation. But still, there was a longing to have someone else bring this Love up in me and mirror it to me. Even when you know the source of Love is in yourself, there can still be a dependency on the other person to be able to see it. I was quite dependent in this way for a long time. I could be in a wonderful relationship and still get frustrated because the other person was not fulfilling all my expectations. Then I would go through the pain of loneliness and of not being seen. It was because I learned how to be with all these difficult feelings and move through them that I eventually found the true Love in myself. It was a challenging journey.

What I eventually found was a different kind of Love that is a pure spaciousness or openness that welcomes everything—all my own pain and the other person exactly as they are. It is a completely different kind of Love than the love we know of as conventional romantic love. It is Love without conditions. It is a Love of whatever is happening in the present. It is openness for life itself.

I had to go through experiencing the pain of separation to touch upon that Love. I could not have experienced that Love just by relating to another person. Another person could not give me that understanding. I had to really go inside myself for that.

LML: Can you share a personal story about this journey?

Carla: For seven years, I had a difficult relationship with a beautiful, poetic, and sensual man. I regarded him as my source of Love and beauty. He had a passionate interest in sacred sexuality and we had wonderful explorations together. But his interest in sex led him to have affairs with many women, which brought up painful feelings in me, like jealousy and rage. As I was present with these difficult feelings, I discovered a lot about my childhood conditioning and how his behavior touched into that. Eventually, it felt so wounding that I could not manage to keep my heart open to him and the relationship ended. I was heartbroken. For months, the radiance of life seemed to have disappeared completely.

One evening, long after our relationship ended, we met briefly for coffee and afterwards I went home feeling absolutely desperate about love again. I had tried so hard and felt that I had failed. I doubted my capacity for love and relating. I found myself distrusting men and my own feelings for them. I could not stop blaming and trying to figure out what I had done wrong, or what he had done wrong.

Suddenly, something in me stopped thinking and stopped judging either him or myself. I sat down and simply felt the substance of the despair itself. I stayed with it. It was very intense. After a while, the desperate and sad feeling in my heart changed into an experience of complete emptiness, which then changed into an experience of space that was clear as a mountain snow. I was surprised! I felt neither the warmth nor the passion in my heart that I had been craving. There was just space and openness. My heart felt like an open window to a crystal-clear sky. It felt just right and very significant.

As I continued to allow this experience to unfold, a delicate friendliness arose and a sense of gratitude for life and a trust and openness for whatever life would bring. For weeks, I remained in the experience of being deeply touched, grateful, tender, and clear. I was loving and open, but without being focused on a particular object, like my former partner. I could say that I discovered the source of Love inside myself at that time. But I also experienced the source of Love to be not only inside myself but *everywhere*.

Shortly after going through this, I met the man who became my husband. Only after going through this fire and discovering the source of Love within myself could I then experience yet another kind of love. This love was a deep appreciation of a unique human being, with his or her personal shine, beauty, and imperfections, without losing contact with the greater Love inherent in all of life. This type of Love became possible as I became less dependent on how the other person appears in any given moment. I was able to be less dependent because

I knew the source of Love inside myself. Then I could let others be exactly how they are.

LML: Yes, true Love is both personal and impersonal. We can appreciate the personal, unique expression of Being that the other is, while at the same time staying in touch with the impersonal, universal Love. Yet we must go through the fire of letting go of grasping at another for Love in order to come to this understanding.

Carla: Very few people have been willing to go through that fire. Life usually has to force us to do it. And, when the love with another inevitably fails to give us the permanent Love we all seek, we often miss that this failure is a doorway to that Love.

LML: It can get covered up quickly by finding another person or distracting ourselves in many ways.

Carla: We want to do anything but be with that pain—anything. But, if the willingness and understanding are there, we can sit with the pain and discover in our own experience that the true Love we all seek is right here under the pain. We need to go through it to know this to be true.

Many books talk about how we can reach that Love—what you should do and what you shouldn't do. In this example, there is still an expectation that the other person would give me the Love only if I knew how to do this or that better.

LML: We can do a lot of rearranging of the story of our conditioning without getting to the ground, the source of infinite Love.

Carla: One thing that I think is difficult about the statement, "Love is not found in another, but in ourselves," is that some people might take that teaching and think that they should stop longing for the other, or that it is not okay to do that. That could become another trip for the ego, which is also part of my personal history. At one point, I came to believe that I don't need anybody in the world. "I'm fine by myself, thank you very much." This creates another separate sense of self. I think it is important to acknowledge that yes, Love is within our self, but Love is also within the other. We are all Love. It is a great joy for two Loves to come together as one. Some people would deny the desire. The desire for two souls meeting in Love might never cease. In the Tantric teachings, we allow the full desire as a force that moves us right through all the layers that obscure true Love.

LML: We don't want to deny the desire for Love with another, and we also do not want to get lost in it. The fine line between the two is allowing everything to be as it is. In that allowing, we find the Love that can be expressed in every moment of life, and in all relationships, including intimate, passionate relationships. Then, we have the freedom to fully play with that and fully enjoy it.

Carla: Yes, I agree. When you can finally just rest in the vast space of your Being, then the fullness of life can move through you in all of its expressions while you remain present. There really is no difference between the experience of space or consciousness and all the full forms of life. It is the oneness of form and emptiness. And, it is possible to use our feelings and bodily sensations as a doorway to the presence of Being by feeling them fully, while at the same time not identifying with them. If we identify with them, they will not lead to the presence of Being, and you will just be overwhelmed by the feelings.

LML: There can be misunderstanding about what is meant by being fully with our feelings. For some people, that means indulging in the feelings, which will not lead to greater presence or Love.

Carla: Yes, and this indulging can be very subtle, incredibly subtle. In order for our feelings and bodily sensations to be doorways to presence, we also need to have some awakened presence to start with. Otherwise, we get lost in our feelings and sensations. The more presence is here, the more fully we can be with what is without identification.

One of the frustrations that I am personally struggling with is letting go of the belief that the other person needs to make me happy.

I know it is not true, but it is a very powerful conditioning and it still comes back sometimes—particularly if I am tired, sad, or overworked. So, I am continuing to digest this truth even more deeply than I did before. We can reconstruct the old ideas very easily. It takes a certain vigilance to watch out for this. We may need to move through it again and again until it is thoroughly understood.

I find relationship to be a powerful teaching. When I am by myself, it is much easier to find the source within. To be very close and intimate with another person and remain conscious and aware of the source of Love without grasping at the other is an enormous challenge. It is important to be gentle with ourselves and appreciate how difficult it can be to wake up out of these deeply conditioned beliefs. In any moment, we have the opportunity to see the belief getting constructed again, and hopefully we just see it without blaming ourselves. We just see the "is-ness" of what is happening and allow more space to unfold.

MEDITATIVE INQUIRY:
You Are the Love You Seek

True Love comes from an infinite source that flows into and through our humanness as our most essential nature. Therefore, we already are the Love we seek. Please take a moment to reflect on the statement, *I already am the Love I seek*. What if you truly knew this, not just intellectually, but through direct knowing beyond doubt? Feel into how knowing that would change the way you are in relationship. I invite you to close your eyes and take some time to contemplate this.

It can be challenging to question the collective myths about romantic relationship that are based on divided love. Looking for love in others is what is familiar. We human beings tend to fear letting go of what is known and familiar and venturing into the unknown to look for deeper truth and solutions. We may also fear that something valuable will be lost by letting go of the familiar version of romantic love. Yet, as Adyashanti (2006–2010), says, "We don't lose the romantic love that we are familiar with when we are awake, we just lose our grasping for it, our attachment to it." Most importantly, letting go of the dream of divided love challenges the existence of a separate, personal identity.

Notice what comes up as you contemplate the statement, "You are the Love you seek." What happens in your body? Is there tension or a deeper relaxation? Is there a fear or doubt? Is there resistance? If so, how is the resistance manifesting? Is there an experience of peace, well-being, and freedom? Just notice what arises without judgment. I invite you to sit with this inquiry repeatedly over time and write down what insights and experiences arise as you contemplate this more deeply.

CHAPTER 2

The Most Important Thing
Awakening to the Source of Love

The most important thing is to find out the most important thing.

—Suzuki Roshi

When Undivided Love is known experientially, it naturally begins to permeate our relationships with its sweet fragrance. This is the essential ingredient for awakened relating. Once the one source of Love is recognized within us, it is a joy to share it with all our other Selves. Then our relating is naturally rooted in Love, rather than in our conditioned mind, which dramatically changes our experience of relationship. Eckhart Tolle (1999) writes, "As humans have become increasingly identified with their mind, most relationships are not rooted in Being and so turn into a source of pain and become dominated by problems and conflict." The more we relate from Being, the more the presence of true Love is expressed through our relating. In this chapter, we will explore *how* to find the source of Love within ourselves, which then makes lasting Love possible in relationships.

The Three Rs of Awakened Relating

To facilitate awakening to true Love, I am offering "The Three Rs" of awakened relating: Recognizing, Resting, and Relying. This is not a method, but rather a simple guideline to assist you in discovering your true nature and then embodying that in relationships and in all of life. There is no formula for awakened relating. It cannot fit entirely into a method, technique, or strategy. Awakened relating arises spontaneously in moments of total acceptance and openness. This relating relies on the infinite intelligence at the core of our Being to provide solutions, rather than our conceptual frameworks and conditioned knowledge.

As we are increasingly free of our stories about our self and others, our relating becomes more spontaneous and naturally appropriate. As we become more awake in our relating, we can let go of our old preconceptions about relationship and our partner that do not serve us. Then, the deeper truth, beauty, and harmony of life can arise, offering true Love and profound benefit. The Three Rs of awakened relating outline the process of discovering awakened Love, which is key to Awakened Relating, and how to live that in relationship. This is a broad outline that is not fixed in time, or in any other way. It is an open-handed offering that speaks to your heart.

Recognizing

Awakening to ever-present Love is more accessible than you might think. In fact, it is immediately available right here and now. We just need to know where and how to look. A simple, practical, and accessible first step in awakening to our true nature is to recognize the ever-present awareness that underlies all experience. This is frequently overlooked as we are focused on the content of awareness rather than awareness itself. Yet, you can simply shift your attention from the ongoing flow of content to the awareness of reading this sentence right now to get a glimpse of what is always present. Our awareness both pervades and includes our experience of reading.

I will share various contemplative inquiries and practices that reveal the uncontrived nature of our Being. These are simple but powerful ways of pointing out our true nature. I will share methods that have worked for me and for others. Although the recognition of our original nature can happen in a multitude of ways, these are ways that have proven effective over time for many people, and they are among the most direct.

SELF-INQUIRY

One way to directly experience our true nature is to turn awareness inward and look at our own direct experience. True inquiry cannot be authentically answered by thought. In the realm of direct experience, beyond or beneath thought, we get a glimpse of awake awareness. This awareness eventually reveals itself to be the presence of pure Love and our own true Self.

In the following inquiry, we observe our own experience of internal phenomena to explore the question: Who am I? Contemplate each question below carefully and use the power of observing awareness to see what is true.

Start with asking, "Am I my thoughts?" Notice that there is something present that is aware of the thoughts.

Then ask, "Am I my feelings?" Be with a feeling and see if you are the feeling or you are the awareness of the feeling.

Inquiring further, ask, "Am I these sensations in my body? Are the ever-changing sensations that make up my experience of the body who I am?"

Looking deeply, can you find anything that separately exists from the awareness in which it is appearing? Notice what is not changing. You are what does not come and go.

The invitation is to relax into the empty space of not knowing and to discover through direct experience the open, knowing presence that is always here. What is the common element in all experience? What is not coming and going? Notice the simple sense of aliveness that comes with the experience of everything arising within. This is the silent answer. Attend to this. Explore this. Become familiar with this.

Another form of self-inquiry, offered by Rupert Spira, a nondual spiritual teacher, begins with our response to the question, "Are you aware?" I invite you to sit with this question right now and simply see that you are aware. This is self-evident. Upon reflection, we can readily see that there is an alert knowing that is always present, but perhaps not always noticed. When this is recognized, we become aware of being aware, or more accurately, awareness becomes conscious of itself. We are not accustomed to seeing and recognizing awareness itself. We are usually attentive only to the objects of awareness—our thoughts, sensations, and perceptions. This simple, open, clear awareness is the ground of our experiences. This is what we need to recognize and return to repeatedly until it has become our default setting.

In *The Natural Bliss of Being* (2013), Jackson Peterson speaks about the inquiry into our true nature.

> If we ask, "Who or what is aware?" or, "Who or what is knowing this experience?" we may discover that we can't find any fixed entity present. We can only find an impersonal con-dition of aware knowing. If we answer, "I am the one who is aware," then we need to ask, "Who or what is aware of this *I* sensation." … Our true nature is what this *I* thought is arising *within*.

It is common to think, "This can't be it." We believe that the nature of our mind must be something more spectacular than ordinary awareness. Because of this, it is often dismissed. Yet, the simple truth is that our Being is aware. Awareness is our essential nature. As we get to know awareness more deeply, we discover that it is an all-powerful, wise, and loving presence. I refer to our ever-present awareness as Undivided Love because it is all-inclusive, all-embracing, fully allow-ing, and it emanates the qualities of benevolence, kindness, and com-passion, among others. The deeper we relax into it, the more we see that "ordinary" awareness is quite extraordinary. The exploration into the nature of this awareness is never-ending as it reveals itself to be not only the source of Love, but also the very substance of all experience.

In addition to using thought to inquire into the nature of mind, we can also stop thinking for a moment so the essence of mind can be recognized. When you pause thought for a moment, what is still present? Is it an empty, blank, nothing? Or, is there an openness that is relaxed, alert, and knowing? This presence is always here, but our constant engagement and identification with thought obscures it. Once this is recognized, we can come to see that it is present, whether thinking is here or not.

Recognition is a two-step process. First, we recognize that this ever-present, pristine awareness is distinct from the thoughts, sensations, and perceptions that appear within it. Once this is clearly seen, our understanding can evolve to the recognition that awareness is not separate from all that appears within it. In fact, aware Beingness pervades all experience. There is nothing that we can think, see, feel, hear, or touch that is separate from our innate capacity to know experience. Yet, our basic awareness is untouched by any experience passing through it.

There is never experience without awareness, nor is there ever awareness without experience. If this inseparability is not recognized, we create another false duality that consists of the imagined "pure" awareness on the one hand and all objects that appear within it on the other. This is only a partial realization and not yet true freedom. However, it is most common to begin with recognizing awareness as distinct from objects, and then our *experiential* understanding can evolve into realizing inseparability or oneness.

Resting

Once we recognize our essential nature, most of us must train in *being* that in our daily lives. Without committing to some form of spiritual training or practice, our recognition can easily be swept away in the continuous and unpredictable flow of the thoughts, feelings, and sensations that we have been conditioned to believe make up who we are and our experience of the world. We certainly will not be able to remain awake in all the intense reactions and emotions that occur in intimate relationship unless we learn to prioritize and emphasize our basic nature in the midst of relating.

Strange as it may seem, our conditioned habit of living as though we are separate from our basic nature is so deeply engrained that we must retrain ourselves to live as what we already are! A Tibetan expression (Sherab and Dongyal 2012) warns us, "Don't leave the teachings on the page of a book." It is equally important to not leave teachings in a talk given by a teacher or on a meditation cushion. *The most effective way to realize our true nature is to simply give it attention, again and again, in the midst of daily life.*

The more settled the mind is, the easier it can be to both recognize our true nature and then rest in or as that nature. We may find resting more difficult if our mind is untamed or disturbed. Therefore, it may be important to do meditation practices that are designed to focus and quiet the mind. Meditation practices can be a significant supplement to the inquiry practices mentioned here. We always have the stability of the breath to return to whenever our mind takes us away from the here and now. A simple practice of focusing on or counting our breath can refocus the mind and bring us back to the here and now. The breath is always in the present moment, which is where we can rest in our deeper awareness again.

I would like to point out that if we *only* do meditation practices without inquiring into our essence, we risk missing the silent, stable nature that is spontaneously present. Yet, if we choose to do nothing and simply say, "There is nothing to do and no one to do it," we also risk never becoming familiar with our natural state, and we may remain identified with our dualistic mind. It is an absolute truth that there is no doer separate from and independent of our essential nature. It is also an absolute truth that we don't have to go anywhere to be what we already essentially are. However, most of us have not yet realized this truth and therefore need to train in awareness until "being aware of being aware" is an ongoing, direct experience in all situations. However, most of us need to train in awareness until "being aware of being aware" is our ongoing, direct experience in all situations.

Recognizing the awareness can be quick, but the process of learning to live *as* that awareness takes time and commitment.

PRACTICING BEING WHAT WE ARE

It is common to do either too much practice, or too little. The only practice that I know of which is neither doing too much nor doing too little is the "non-practice" of resting *as* awareness. I received this instruction from Adyashanti (2012), who teaches that, "Meditation is the art of *allowing everything to simply be* in the deepest possible way. … It is most fundamentally an *attitude of being*—a resting in and as *being*. … True Meditation is *effortless stillness, abidance as primordial being.*" The emphasis here is on *being* awareness rather than on being aware of the objects that arise in awareness.

Adyashanti (2006) further teaches that, "Resting your attention, relaxing your attention into this presence of awareness, the sense of it, the feel of it, the openness of it, the mystery of it. This is what you can do. … To rest in this utter simplicity is itself the highest spiritual practice."

My experience of pure awareness quickly deepened when I discovered the "effortless practice" of resting as awareness for short moments repeated many times until it became continuous. Once recognized, we rest attention in the changeless awareness rather than fixate on the contents of awareness. Resting involves being present to the immediate now with open receptivity without comment, agenda, or demand. It is not about doing anything, it is *being* awareness itself. We simply rest as naked awareness for as long as the moment lasts before the mind takes us away again into thought.

The Dzogchen master, Tulku Urgyen Rinpoche, was the first to introduce me to this pinnacle practice that has helped human beings realize and stabilize the nature of mind for centuries. In my personal experience, the practice of short moments of resting as awareness in relationship can support the practice of awakened relating more than anything else. With consistent dedication, the short moments become longer until resting in our natural state is the predominant experience. As Tulku Urgyen (2000) states, "Remain in uncontrived naturalness for short moments repeated many times. You *can* become accustomed to this. The short moment *can* grow longer." This is how we can build our capacity to be in the here and now.

Focusing on the deepest sense of our self that we can access in any moment is a path home to true Love, our natural state. Being self-aware in this way is always available to everyone. It is the simplest and most effective way.

If it seems as though you do not have access to a deeper sense of yourself in any given moment, then you can rest by simply relaxing the body and mind to the best of your ability. Relax out of the mind and into the heart or the belly. Just taking a moment to drop out of the stories in the head and focus on the sensations in the body is a move-ment towards a deeper truth. It is through relaxed openness infused with curiosity and wonder that our awareness comes more clearly into view. We *relax* into noticing Love's presence.

RAISING YOUR VIBRATION

In addition to relaxing out of the mind and into the heart or body, you can simply focus your attention on whatever gives you joy, excite-ment, or peace. That can be anything—a positive thought or image and the feeling it brings, looking at a tree in the sunlight from the window, feeling the breeze on your face, or sensing into the warmth of a purring cat on your lap. Shifting our energy vibration to a higher frequency such as joy, excitement, or peace more closely approximates our natural state and therefore makes it more accessible. We access our deeper nature from openness, not from contracted states of mind.

EARTH-BASED PRACTICES

For some, returning to our natural connection with the Earth is what best facilitates both recognizing and relying on true nature. Even if we are more drawn to the practices described above, it is important for all of us who are awakening out of the dream of separation to return to our connection with nature. We have become increasingly out of touch with the natural world. Instead, we are living mostly indoors and in front of computers, smartphones, or TV screens. Human beings are part of nature on this planet; we are never actually separate from it. To live as though we are separate is unnatural and unhealthy. Awakened relating includes all of life. We are always in relationship with everything. If we relate to nature as something separate from us, we cannot relate to our other Selves in a connected way.

The natural world is a direct expression of the essence of Being prior to the confines of words, doctrines, and concepts. Being immersed in nature can bring us back in touch with who we were before all of our habitual tendencies, cultural influences, and conditioning took over. Nature is already one with all that is, untouched by our beliefs in separation and division. If we are open and willing, nature will reveal our natural oneness with all of life. The Earth itself is a living, breathing display of the living Love that life is.

Earth Meditation.   Allow nature to point you back to your own true nature by sitting on the Earth with an open heart. It is best to sit directly on the ground and put your bare feet in touch with the Earth, if possible. Remain still, allowing your eyes to receive the whole visual field at once with a wide-angle vision. If the mind wanders, gently bring the attention back to the stillness of a tree, the vast expanse of the sky, the sounds of birds, or the fluidity of water. Blend with these living expressions of the qualities of essence.

To open into a wide-angle vision that includes the periphery, but is not focused on anything in particular, settles the mind and opens the heart. When we blend with and receive whatever the world is presenting to us in this way, it cuts through the blaring noise of our mind, bringing at least a moment of relief and relaxation. In addition to sitting in nature, softening and widening our gaze can be used any time as a way of taking a short moment or to shift out of our fixation on mind-states.

I am offering these practices and methods of self-inquiry as skillful means for awakening to our nature and embodying that in relationship. If you already recognize your true nature and have a way to support and train in stabilizing this—great! If you don't, then try out these suggestions and explore the experiences they evoke. The biggest challenge with all the simple instructions mentioned here is to stick to them with great diligence. If you do, you cannot fail to discover the true source of Love and begin to live that in relationship.

Relying

Once we have recognized our essential nature, we can return to it again and again, which allows it to grow stronger. We can then rely on this deeper wisdom to provide all solutions to what troubles us. The more we rely on that wisdom, the more we will learn to trust the natural flow of life, and the more it will inform our relating. We come to see that it is the source of all Love, wisdom, happiness, safety, and security. There is no other source. Everything else is a conceptual phantom that comes and goes and does not provide any lasting change or well-being. We can either rely on the source of all solutions or go to the conditioned mind and rummage through the trash of our repetitive thoughts for a solution, which at best will be limited and temporary. The truth is that all good ideas always emerge from our openness to the mystery.

Please note that our minds can create endless complexities and confusions out of these simple instructions. Therefore, I invite you to seriously consider finding a clear guide or teacher to assist you in the process of awakening and embodiment, if you don't already have one. I cannot emphasize the importance of this enough! I have found my teachers to be an invaluable and necessary part of my spiritual journey. We all have to walk our path alone, but clear guides can help us stay on the path, and keep us from getting lost in spiritual concepts and confusion. It is important to pay attention to how much a teacher has embodied their awakening. Remember, it is possible to be quite awake and still not be embodied in relationships or other areas of life.

The couples whose stories and conversations I share this book are each experiencing awakened relating in their own way. Some are practicing short moments, and some are not. Some have a deep, abiding realization of awakened awareness, and for some it appears to come and go. Michael and Catherine are an example of practicing relaxing for short moments into the spaciousness of Being in the midst of their relating.

Awakened relating is so nascent in human experience that we are all pioneers exploring this new frontier together. Intimate relationship is one of the best training grounds for both discovering real, Undivided Love and for embodying it. Intimate relationship continually brings up all the ways we believe in separation, all our points of view about ourselves and others, and our relational wounding. Intimacy offers a powerful opportunity for awakening. As I have heard Adyashanti say many times in various talks, "Relationship is where the spiritual rubber meets the road."

Practicing Awakened Relating

Michael and Catherine: Practicing Short Moments in Relationship

Michael and Catherine met in a spiritual community over twenty years ago and have been focused spiritually throughout their entire relationship, sharing a deep longing to fully realize what is most true. As Catherine says, "It is our primary commitment in life." They discovered awakened relating through the practice of resting for short moments in the relaxed openness at the basis of all experience. This allows them to be with whatever arises between them in relationship with wisdom, compassion, and clarity.

What follows here is a conversation I had with them as they share their experience with practicing short moments and how this has guided them through relational ups and downs. Michael begins the conversation by giving an example of an incident that brought up resistance in him and how resting and relying on a deeper wisdom brought a natural resolution.

Michael: Catherine likes to keep the house cleaner than I would do on my own. She recently wanted to clean the house and I immediately went into resistance, which is quite common with this activity, and I stood in that position quite firmly. When she asked me to do the cleaning, I burst out with a sarcastic comment that I knew was inappropriate, but it just came rolling out. I started doing the cleaning anyway and noticed a strong resistance. I began doing short moments of resting in the underlying awareness. It was so amazing because then all of the tight, angry energy that was filling my thoughts about how ridiculous it was to have to keep everything so clean just suddenly opened up.

Throughout our entire relationship, I've acted out a pattern of internally resisting doing the cleaning but doing it anyway with a lot of unexpressed resentment. I allowed my angry, resentful, and self-justifying thoughts to be there, "as is," while relaxing into short moments of noticing that which is aware of these thoughts and feelings. The thoughts and emotions would quiet down and then come back again and I would do another short moment, then the emotions would rise up, and another short moment. After about five minutes of this, BOOM, all of that energy I was running through that loop suddenly opened up and became completely available to do the cleaning. It was like I was a tornado. There wasn't anything else I wanted to do. It was totally delightful. I just put my whole self into it naturally. Within minutes, this long-term pattern was completely different. Something as mundane as cleaning the house became a doorway into my essential nature! I've seen that it's not just when we set aside time to meditate, it's in every moment of ordinary life.

LML: Yes, this is a very important point—our essential nature is the basic state pervading every moment of daily life. We don't have to look any further than that to find it. It's not in a special place. It is right here in whatever is happening now.

Catherine: I will share that Michael has an extremely keen intellect and he will use that to make himself right. I do short moments when I see that arise in him and I experience the sweetest laugh because I now see "cuteness" in it—the tenaciousness of a little boy. I have had a fundamental shift in my perspective on Michael since doing the practice of short moments. I see him from such a place of gratitude and appreciation and not from the old ways of needing him to be like this and not like that, which was my common perspective in the past. I am a fastidious person, so it can be difficult living with me, no question. However, I am no longer hit by mind streams about him needing to be different than he is. I am not only allowing him to be as he is, I am now really appreciating who he is and seeing his gifts in ways I couldn't see before.

Michael: When I have been in the darkest places in our relationship, even thinking that the relationship is not going to make it. ... When my deeper nature opens up through repeated resting as awareness, what occurs is that all the boundaries between us just dissolve. We are simply both participating in Love. I have never before felt such a total sense of Love for Catherine, it goes beyond the personal love for her but includes that love as well. This Love is just the sweetest, most intimate experience. When I do the short moments, I experience something so much deeper than ever before. The experience of falling in Love and all the deepest emotions of "Catherine is the one," really don't hold a candle to this experience of complete infinite Love that comes when that short moment opens up the energy of a disturbing state. Disturbing states, which I previously avoided at almost any cost in my relationship, have now naturally become doorways into the deeper meaning of Love and relationship for me.

LML: Thank you Michael, that is quite profound. We tend to seek the highs of relationship, such as falling in love, and push away all the uncomfortable or painful states that inevitably arise in relationship. Yet when we rest in these uncomfortable experiences, rather than avoid them, they open up into a Love even greater than the "highs" of romantic love. This is a beautiful example of awakened relating.

Michael: When I first learned short moments, I was instructed to just stop thinking for a moment and notice what's here. I experienced clarity and I felt an energy. This reminded me of what I experienced when I used to meditate with TM, and now it's like, "Oh, look at that!" I can just go directly there in any moment in the midst of my life. I always have access to that openness and spaciousness. So, now after some time of practicing this, all I have to do is to think, "Oh, take a short moment," and it's right here. In the midst of a strong emotion like anger, I can have the intention to do a short moment, even if I am still awash in all the strong emotional energy. I keep reminding myself to take a short moment and the intention seems to eventually break through the confines of that emotional stream. The energy opens up and I am no longer caught in it. I am no longer at the mercy of my feelings, sensations, or circumstances. All that is secondary and suddenly I am in complete control of my life. I am not a victim of it anymore.

Sometimes strong feelings, such as anger, are still there, but instead of that being my whole focus and overwhelming me, it's no longer the driving force. I haven't gotten rid of this energy, or emotional state, but it is no longer the predominant experience. In the past, when anger would take over, I was so at the mercy of it; anger totally had me. Then, I was afraid I was going to express it and be inappropriate with Catherine. And, also, there was such confusion. As I repeatedly relax into my Being, feelings and reactions might still be occurring, but now they are in the midst of what I can call spaciousness. Feelings no longer control my experience, so I no longer have fear of being inappropriate and acting out in relationship. I can just be who I naturally am.

MEDITATIVE INQUIRY:
Awakening to Love's Source

I invite you to select one of the ways of recognizing the source of Love that I offered, or one of your own, and contemplate it as often as possible until you recognize your own natural state. It is always helpful to get the support of clear spiritual teachers who can point you to this truth.

When doing inquiry, allow the body to be comfortable and relax the mind, but remain alert. Remember that the thinking mind can't take us to realization. The purpose of inquiries is to take us to the recognition of silent awareness, not to more thought.

Notice the qualities of Love in the relaxed openness at the basis of all experience. It can be referred to as Love because it embraces all, includes all, and resists nothing. See for yourself if you can find any resistance to "what is" without going to the mind. Is the awareness itself resisting anything? Be curious, relaxed, and joyful in these investigations.

Once you have recognized your basic nature, train in *being* that in your daily life and relationships. This recognition becomes the path and the practice. My suggestion is to recognize the basic nature again and again by relaxing *as* that for short (or long) moments during whatever is occurring in your life. Let it all be while noticing and emphasizing the ground of Being from which it all arises.

This can also be practiced even if you do not yet have clear recognition of your true nature by simply relaxing the mind into the heart and breathing into the belly for repeated moments. Pay attention to moments of peace or quiet. Dedication to this will lead to a deeper recognition.

If you are moved to, set aside time to practice meditation by focusing on the breath until the mind is more calm and quiet and then practice resting repeatedly in the deeper silent awareness below thought. If the mind pulls you away, lovingly focus on the breath again without judgment until you can return to focusing on awareness again. This will greatly enhance your ability to recognize, rest, and rely.

CHAPTER 3

The Accepting Heart
Awakening Self-Love

*Do you normally hold yourself in low esteem? To correct your
view, all you need to do is to understand your true nature, the
way you already are. That's all. It's so simple.*

—Lama Thubten Yeshe

Awakened relating begins with true self-love, which is fully allowing
and accepting all of who we are, just as we are, in the open embrace of
Undivided Love. Self-love naturally flows from self-knowledge. Getting
to know ourselves intimately in this way is a necessary foundation for
true intimacy. The more we come to directly know the all-inclusive
perfection of our deeper nature, the more we can love and accept all
the human expressions of this nature, including our apparent limitations and flaws. Then our perfect true nature can illumine our imperfect human nature. We can more fully love our self the more we
recognize who we really are.

Our primary relationship is with ourselves. We are not able to
receive love when we believe we are unlovable. We cannot fully accept
others if we cannot accept ourselves. We cannot truly know others if
we do not know ourselves. We cannot offer genuine caring and compassion to others if we relate to our self with harshness, judgment, and
criticism. Since we are not actually separate from others, our relationship with our self affects our relationships, and can block the flow of
Love.

True self-love includes an intimate meeting of all our human expressions in the form of thoughts, feelings, sensations, behaviors, qualities, and personality. When none of that is made wrong or imagined to be other than our essence, it takes its rightful place at home in pure, Undivided Love. All aspects of what we believe ourselves to be— positive, negative, and neutral—have the same all-loving essence. This essence is revealed when we allow everything to be *as it is* without resisting or following it.

If we are not allowing this intimate meeting, it will create division within us and in relationship. All the unseen, rejected parts of us will inevitably appear in intimate relationship. If we remain unconscious, we will project those unaccepted parts onto our partner. *We blame and attack others for what we cannot see or accept in ourselves.* Then we try to fix our partner on whom we have projected our deeply buried or rejected parts. This will cause relational disharmony until we take responsibility and meet all these rejected parts with unconditional acceptance. When we do this, it frees up a lot of energy for simply enjoying each other and sharing the Love that we most essentially are.

As we come more into our true identity, we begin to see ourselves through the eyes of infinite Love, rather than through the distorted lens of our learned beliefs and judgments. Yet, without this understanding, it is far too common for human beings to be caught in a painful web of self-hatred, which appears to obscure our natural state. Many of us suffer with the belief that we do not deserve love. However, no matter what we were taught, or how unacceptable we think we are, we all deserve to be loved and know ourselves as Love. It is also true that it goes beyond deserving because Undivided Love is an unconditional grace that redeems us without any deserving involved. The feeling of not deserving is so prevalent in our society that I would like to inquire into the origins of this self-hatred.

The Belief That We Are Flawed

Self-rejection is rampant in our world. The pressure is everywhere. We feel we are never quite living up to the high standards presented to us by our parents, our culture, our peers, and the commercial media. We're never attractive or thin enough, have a nice enough home, or a big enough bank account. We are pressured to acquire and achieve. On top of that, we have the conditioning of our childhood. Parenting in the West has largely been based on punishment and control. For too many, the emphasis has been on having obedient children who are controlled as opposed to encouraging them to blossom into their natural gifts and abilities. As children, we are often not loved for who we are, but for what we achieve or how well we conform and obey. This is true for many Eastern cultures as well.

As children, many of us heard messages such as, "What's wrong with you? Can't you do anything right?" In addition, many of us also had other forms of relational wounding or trauma, which will be explored in Chapters 5 and 6. Relational wounding leaves us with beliefs such as, "I'm not good enough" or "I'm unlovable." It is not surprising that many of us came to believe that something is wrong with us. I remember feeling that there was something wrong with me at my core. That feeling was so pervasive and deep that I couldn't imagine ever being free of it. Yet, today I know from experience that it is possible to break free from self-hatred through coming to know the beauty and perfection of our shared true nature.

In addition to the conditioning we receive in our family, there is a widespread, collective belief that all human beings are fundamentally flawed. In fact, our negative conditioning arises out of that belief and it is continually reinforced. In the West, this may come from the story of Adam and Eve and original sin. In the East, it may be about the belief in karma. In both cases, we are taught that something is essentially wrong with us, and we have to atone for it. This produces a sense of unworthiness based on an *inherent* flaw. The myth that we are defective is as pervasive and unquestioned as the myth that Love is found outside of our self. It is another aspect of our collective unconscious that needs to be explored in order for us to see that there is actually no truth to it. It is vitally important to carefully examine the belief that we are inherently flawed because it contaminates the relationship with our self, and therefore with others.

Even deeper than the belief we are inherently flawed is the belief that we are separate from Love, each other, and from nature. The belief that we are flawed, along with all other self-negativity, emerges out of the belief in separation. Nonseparation, or unity, is the fundamental truth of life. If that truth is not experientially known, there will be a sense that something is wrong or lacking. One interpretation of the Adam and Eve story is that the original sin was stepping out of oneness with God and into an apparent duality of good and evil, and therefore separation. Before that occurred, Adam and Eve lived in harmony and unity in the Garden of Eden. We all leave a paradise that resides within us each time we step into duality. We are then viewing life through a fundamental misperception of reality, which can't possibly bring the Love and happiness we seek.

When we believe we are flawed, we experience ourselves to be merely a tiny speck of the vast perfection that we truly are. We all have the potential to more fully manifest the infinite beauty and power of our wholeness, rather than contract into a small fraction of that. We put limitations and boundaries on ourselves with beliefs such as, "I'm not good enough" or "I'm unlovable." These self-imposed limitations are like the ocean believing itself to be one drop of water, unable to sense its vastness. No matter how insecure we may feel from the vantage of the divided self, in truth, we are immense beyond imagination.

The Fallacy of the Self-Improvement Project

We all want to love and accept our self, but may not know how. For a long time, I didn't know how to love myself. From the perspective of the separate identity, I saw self-improvement as the only way to become loveable. Before I learned what true self-love was, I dedicated my life to the self-improvement project. All my time and resources went into that. I was determined to cure my self-hatred by healing and improving all my wounds and flaws. I was plagued by a sense of unworthiness and insecurity, constantly comparing myself to others and feeling "less than." This suffering propelled me to look deeper and find a way to be free of it.

Therapeutic healing work helped me build a foundation for awakening. It was an important part of my process, but somehow, I knew that this healing alone was not enough to free me from the limited identity that imprisoned me. There was an inner voice with quiet strength that kept urging me to keep going deeper. This led me to become involved with the spiritual self-improvement project. At first, this was an attempt to transcend my "flawed self." When this also failed, it was a saving grace. It eventually led me to discover the effortless self-love of simply allowing all of who I am to be exactly as it is in the naturally loving presence of awareness, moment to moment. I came to see that I simply needed to see that my negative self-image was not the truth of who I am.

It is important to point out that accepting yourself as you are does not mean never working on or improving yourself. If we have wounding and trauma that interferes with our life, it is important to do healing work with that. If we have addictions or other habits that are harmful to us or others, then it is important to address that. Awakening alone will not resolve these issues, but knowing our essential okay-ness makes their full resolution possible. Knowing the ground of Being is the necessary foundation for true self-acceptance and healing.

The key is making improvements from a place of acceptance. We begin with self-love. We start with the acceptance that can only come from our essential nature, which means always unconditionally accepting all that is. It may sound backwards to the conditioned mind to start with acceptance, but it is the gentlest, most effective way to bring about lasting change. Sometimes this happens instantly, and sometimes it takes repeated moments of dropping into the unconditional acceptance of our Being over time to dissolve long-standing, negative self-beliefs. But, it really is that simple.

However, when we strive for improvement from a place of non-acceptance, it becomes endless and futile. Cheri Huber (2001) asks, "Can you stop trying to change into who you wish you were long enough to find out who you really are? You will never improve yourself enough to meet your standards. Egocentricity will see to that. But the moment you love yourself, you are completely changed." Our separate ego identity does not want you to accept yourself as you are. Since the ego identity is a thought that believes it is a self, it wants to survive. One of the main ways it survives is by keeping us believing that something is wrong with us and that we need to keep working on fixing what is wrong. When we accept our self as we are, all that falls apart and so does the separate self.

True awakening and transformation can only happen in the full meeting of all the *seemingly* broken parts of us at their source and ground. This is not a meeting of two things; it is the dissolution of the appearance of two. The ground of Love does not bypass all our flawed and wounded parts, leaving them behind. True Love heals by embracing them all in complete acceptance and revealing them to be Love masquerading as flaws!

Self-Love Begins With Self-Knowledge

If loving our self is not about self-improvement, what is it about? First and foremost, it is about self-knowledge. How can we love our self if we do not even know who we truly are? When asked the question, "Who are you," most people will answer in terms of their gender, race, work, hobbies, interests, family, and so on. For example, I might say, "I am a woman, mother, wife, psychotherapist, and meditator." I think we all have a sense that we are more than these things, but we may not know what that is, or how to find it. In the previous chapter, we explored ways to inquire into our true identity. It is well worth the effort and attention required to look beyond our roles and our surface identity to see what is most true about who we are.

If we look closely and sincerely, we actually do not find the limited, flawed self that we believe ourselves to be. We find a presence of openness, spaciousness, and knowing. We are actually more of a spacious presence than a person. As we settle into that, we sense that we are something that is much more vast, unlimited, and inherently good. This discovery naturally can lead to self-acceptance that is not based on what we look like or what we do. It is based on the deeper knowing of what is already perfectly okay at our core, regardless of how our conditioned self appears.

As we get to know the simple openness of our Being, it's revealed that we are *naturally* loving and kind. We don't have to change a single thing about our self to be loveable. We are inherently precious and loveable. We simply need to see the truth of who we are. As this becomes known, all efforts to change can relax. In this relaxation, everything that needs to change will either naturally release, or we will be given the wisdom and strength to make the changes.

Even if our flaws don't fall away, we no longer identify with or act on them once they have been met with unconditional acceptance. Therefore, they are no longer a concern. They may still arise, but our relationship to them has changed. We can receive them with openness and kindness. They are allowed to arise and fall back into the source from which they came. Then, all of the massive amount of energy that was once put into our self-improvement project can be put into being of genuine benefit to our self and each other.

When we are fully identified with the divided self, then our self-esteem rises and falls with what is going on with our body and mind. We will be forever riding that roller coaster if we do not know our essential nature. As our identity shifts from being the body, mind, and personality to being pure presence, we can relax into a deep acceptance of our self as we are. This allows us to begin living as the magnificent and unique blessing that we each are.

Seeing through the eyes of our true heart—that which is untouched by our wounding—is very healing and transformative. This seeing is not imagination, nor is it coming from the conditioned mind. It is real and true, and therefore has the power to transform our wounds. Once we get a glimpse of the Love that is at the core of our Being, we can never fully believe the self-hating voice again. It will be forever challenged. Then, even when it appears again, we know through direct experience, not from belief, that the negative sense of self is not all there is and it is not what is most essentially true. This makes it possible to begin to let it go.

It can't be emphasized enough how important it is to treasure a glimpse of our true nature by returning to it for brief moments as often as possible. We become interested, curious, and committed to it. This is how the glimpse can grow into a constant, lived realization. Otherwise, a glimpse can get lost in the torrents of the conditioned mind and we never know when we will be graced with one again. It must first be recognized, and then rested in and relied on in relationship and in all of life.

Practicing Awakened Relating

Jamie: Awakening From the Dream of "I'm Not Good Enough"

Jamie does not present as someone who is insecure. He is highly successful and has many positive qualities. Yet, he absolutely believed that he was not good enough. Jamie lived in a family of high achievers who valued achievement over who you are as a person. His self-worth and self-image were formed around his significant achievements. If he didn't achieve, he was met with harsh criticism from his father.

Jamie was successful at sports and everything else he did in school, and now has a successful career. He was extremely dependent on this success for a sense of self-worth and safety, and if he ever made a mistake or failed in any way, Jamie became terrified that the mistake proved he was not good enough. Even the smallest failure made Jamie very anxious. He later understood that this was because it triggered memories of the harsh treatment from his critical father, which had traumatized him as a child.

Jamie had difficulty with intimacy because he did not want to open up to someone deeply enough for them to discover his imagined inadequacy. He remained somewhat closed off and distanced from his wife, which resulted in relational disharmony and conflict. Jamie could not imagine being loved for who he is, since this was outside his conditioned experience. Therefore, he avoided close contact and was rarely truly present in relation to others. He was more comfortable focusing on work than on relationships.

Not only was Jamie not present with others, he also was not present with himself. He rarely took time to relax and be with himself. He was always on the go, mostly working at his demanding career. Even when not working, Jamie was always busy *doing*, and rarely just *being*. He often rushed from one activity to another to avoid even just a few minutes of being still. He was aware of a voice inside that told him to slow down and relax, but he did he know how to do that, so he didn't listen.

Then life hit him over the head—literally. As a result of a bicycle accident during a race, Jamie suffered a head injury that resulted in a serious concussion. Jamie's life as he knew it came to an abrupt halt. The doctor instructed him not to read or look at a screen on any device. He could only listen to audio recordings for short periods of time. Worst of all, he could not work. Someone who could not stop and be with himself for a minute was now faced with himself every waking moment, with very little distraction. It only took a little more than a week of this before he reached out and contacted me in a panic asking for support. Jamie reported that he was alone with nothing but his "demon" and no way to escape it. The demon was his self-hatred that manifested as a persistent belief that he was never good enough. Along with that came all the traumatic memories and feelings associated with this negative conditioning, which he had never allowed himself to feel.

As fate would have it, meditation provided the most relief from the headaches caused by his concussion. Jamie learned to meditate by listening to guided meditation recordings. If he had too many thoughts, especially negative, worrisome thoughts, his head would pound with pain and his anxiety would spike. He was literally forced to learn to relax and quiet his mind.

Formerly, he had been unable to tolerate a weekend meditation retreat he attended years ago. Now he had no choice but to be on extended retreat. Fortunately, Jamie was open to seeing this situation in the bigger context of the potential transformation it offered. He knew that he needed to learn to slow down, and he wanted to transform his belief that he is not good enough. This belief had controlled his life, and he knew it. Now, he had nothing to do but face it and see it for what it really is, and move beyond it.

With my support, daily meditation, and listening to talks by spiritual teachers who point to our true identity, Jamie developed a mindful awareness that allowed him to see the thoughts, feelings, and sensations associated with self-hatred. They came up often, as he was feeling completely inadequate for not being able to do his job during a busy time when they needed him. This caused him to feel like a total failure, even though he had a very good reason for not doing his job. He was actually incapable of working at the time due to his injury.

The negative thoughts and feelings about himself became something Jamie was conscious of and looking *at*, rather than something he was. As he said, "I'm over here, and it's [self-hatred] over there." For the first time in his life, he experienced some distance from the self-negativity. At one point, in a moment of openness when Jamie's mind was quiet, I pointed to the awareness that was observing the thoughts and feelings. I suggested noticing that this awareness was the one constant, the only thing that was not coming and going. Fortunately, Jamie was able to directly recognize the ever-present awareness. He became "aware of being aware."

In the beginning, he was merged with the contents of the mind, and he then became mindfully aware of the content. Now, there was awareness of the awareness that all contents were appearing within. This provided Jamie with the opportunity to return to that repeatedly by resting his attention in that underlying awareness. Each time the negative self-talk arises, he has an opportunity to become aware of it and rest as the awareness that is unaffected by the thoughts and see that they simply dissolve.

Upon further inquiry, Jamie discovered that his "not good enough" self-image was dissolved in the moments when he rested as awareness. In those moments, he could not find an inadequate self. He only found an abiding peaceful presence. Jamie had nothing to do but be with this process that had become his primary focus and priority. He had never felt so relaxed in his life, and he did not want to lose that. In his words, "Never before have I not been ruled by insecurity. Never before have I been in so much peace." He did not want to return to being driven by self-hatred and fear and the need to achieve. He also did not want to return to the isolation that came along with distancing himself from those closest to him.

Now, when asked if he believes he is not good enough, he laughs and says, "That is only a thought and I am not my thoughts. I can see the belief, 'I'm not good enough,' but I have distance from it and I'm not entering into it. I see it along with the tension it creates in my body, and just question it and let it go. That either happens right away, or more and more quickly after getting caught in it. Then, I relax again into the larger space of awareness that I am. I am no longer fully identified with the voice in my head. In the past, it just gripped me and felt completely true. Now, I am able to question my negative self-talk and let it go."

The relaxation of this pattern of belief has allowed Jamie to open up to his wife in a way he never had before. He was no longer afraid of her seeing an imagined, flawed self. Jamie began to experience closeness and intimacy in relationship for the first time. His wife's openhearted response to this allowed him to experience being loved for who he is, in the deepest sense, rather than for his achievements. His new relational availability was also healing for his wife, since she had grown up with an emotionally unavailable father. As Jamie says, "I am now free to love and be loved without having to always keep a part of me hidden that I believed to be unlovable."

Life gave Jamie a crash course in transforming self-hatred. He went from fully believing his negative opinions about himself to seeing the deepest truth of who he is in a relatively short period of time. His old patterns continue to emerge. It is an on-going process of being mindfully aware of the patterns when they appear and returning again and again to the new understanding. By doing so, his self-hatred is being transformed at its root. Rather than making a lot of effort to shift his negative beliefs about himself to positive beliefs, which can't be done in a lasting way, Jamie is realizing the illusory nature of all belief. His concussion was the catalyst, but his openness and commitment to the discovery of his true nature is what transformed the negative beliefs he held about himself. When we sincerely want to know the deepest truth, life will provide us with whatever experience is needed to make that possible. If it needs to hit us over the head literally or figuratively, it will—whatever it takes. We are all given exactly what we need.

MEDITATIVE INQUIRY:
Practicing Acceptance

For just one day, or for at least one hour, practice accepting yourself as you are. Be mindfully aware of how many times you criticize yourself or "should" yourself. Notice what your thoughts tell you about yourself. Notice how you *feel* about yourself. Be mindful of the self-judgments and just see them in compassionate awareness. Feel the sensations in your body. Allow whatever arises to just be, the best you can.

Next, practice accepting your partner, or any other person, as they are for one day, or at least one hour. Be aware of how many times you resist who they are or how they behave. Notice when you contract around something they say or do. Are you able to just notice the contraction in compassionate awareness, or do you say something to them about how they should be different than they are? Can you accept them fully before saying anything? If there is total acceptance *first*, then we have the clarity to know what to say or do, if needed.

You might be surprised at how often there is non-acceptance of yourself and others. This is also an exercise in self-honesty. Please see this with self-compassion as you continue to increase your awareness.

CHAPTER 4

The Madness of the Gods
Falling in Love

There is really no such thing as falling in or out of love.
That is a total illusion. It's a misnomer.
You can fall in and out of attraction, but not love.
Love is always present.

—Adyashanti

When we fall in love, we are given an invaluable opportunity to see the ever-present Love in our beloved partner and know that it is a mirror of the same Love within us. It is a magical, sometimes fleeting glimpse that allows us to open our heart essence and touch the true Love that we long for so deeply. When we access this Love, we transcend the judgments and beliefs that separate us. Our self-obsession is temporarily suspended, and in that, we find tremendous relief. Falling in love offers us a precious glimpse of undivided, unconditional Love. When we fall in love, we are actually in love with Love itself, not just the person.

By falling in love, we are able to experience moments, if not longer periods, when our deepest underlying angst caused by believing that we are separate from Love and from others is suspended. All of the grasping that normally underlies everything we do can subside into a relaxed acceptance. Finally, we can rest for a while.

The unity we have searched for all our lives is found in these moments. It could be said that Love *is* the absence of the sense of separation. We can all look at our own experience and see that the experience of falling in love is a kind of merging or union that dissolves our sense of being separate from one another. The imagined separation was always mind-made. When that facade falls away, the experience of Love is naturally revealed; it is what remains.

Falling in love can be a treasured experience of being seen by another in an adoring way. For some of us, it may be for the first time since our mother's loving gaze when we were babies. For others, it may be the very first time that anyone has looked at them with loving eyes. This can be so healing for the human body, mind, and heart. At last, we are seen. It can also allow us to experience being fully in the present moment, which is rare for most of us. Being in love can consume our consciousness and keep attention from straying elsewhere. We are experiencing what we have always wanted; there is nowhere else we want to go. There may only be moments of this, but these are powerful, transcendent moments.

When we first fall in love, we are able to accept the other person fully; they appear to be perfect. We don't focus on their apparent faults, annoying habits, and negative traits. What we clearly see is the beauty of their Being. When we are under the spell of being in love, we accept and even find endearing our beloved's annoying habits that may often drive us crazy later. For each of us, being in the presence of someone who unconditionally accepts us is a very powerful experience. It opens our heart to our true Self and all of life. For many, falling in love is the pinnacle experience of life because it touches the infinite.

Falling in love can feel so magical and so out of the ordinary because it transports us beyond our limited sense of self. We enter into a much larger, openhearted way of being that is free from the burdens of our ego's defenses and self-obsession. This Undivided Love is all-inclusive and embraces all of our divided self without being identified with it. We get a taste of true freedom and true Love. Yet, it is only a taste. The extent to which we understand the deeper truth of what is happening when we fall in love makes all the difference in whether it will deepen and last or become a memory that we long for.

In that delicious beginning of falling in love, there is an unconditional openness that happens effortlessly. We are given a freebie. It feels so timeless and real, so true to our nature and effortless. Yet, in the opening that Undivided Love creates, it is inevitable that our conditioning, insecurities, and fears will reappear to be met in that Love. If we resist at this point, then the Love will no longer seem effortless, and it appears to be divided. We have the important opportunity and choice to deepen and mature Love by embracing all our experience, including the painful insecurities and fears. The arising of these experiences is not evidence that Love has been lost. True Love can never be lost. They are arising to be met and healed in the presence of Undivided Love as our capacity to *be* Love blossoms.

When Love Appears Divided

If this glimpse of our heart essence is followed wisely, it can lead to the discovery that Love is always here. Undivided Love includes the "object" of our love, but is not limited to that. It exists as our natural state and can be experienced independent of any object. Unfortunately, this Love is usually projected onto the object of love alone. We believe the object of our love is the source of Love. Therein lies the problem that will inevitably divide us. This is the misunderstanding that underlies all relationship struggles. As soon as we step into relating as an imagined, separate someone who is getting love from another separate someone, it is inevitable that trouble will arise.

When we believe the source of Love is "over there," an ultimately unworkable, dysfunctional pattern comes into play in either subtle or overt ways. In the more intense expressions of this confusion, we become strongly attached to the imagined source and cling to it for fear of losing it. The fear of loss may also lead us to attempt to control and manipulate the other or ourselves. We may distort our self into what the other wants, withholding our truth and ignoring our boundaries. This misunderstanding can also cause us to become addicted to and obsessed with the object of our love. In extreme cases, we may attack or even kill the other when we imagine that the source of Love is being taken away from us. Falling in love can evolve into an ever-increasing love affair with all of life or it can devolve into a dysfunctional obsession. Eckhart Tolle (2005) explains the difference between addictive love and true Love:

> What is commonly called "falling in love" is in most cases an intensification of egoic wanting and needing. You become addicted to another person, or rather to your image of that person. It has nothing to do with true love, which contains no wanting whatsoever.

Searching for Lasting Happiness in Relationship

When we believe we are a divided self, we are always searching for happiness. The movement to seek happiness arises out of the dissatisfaction inherent in feeling separate. It's true that a new lover can temporarily stimulate happiness through getting what we desire. For a brief time, our chronic grasping at what we want is suspended. In the absence of grasping, our deeper Being naturally shines forth and *that* is the experience of happiness.

If we know how to look, each moment that is free of seeking is an opportunity to recognize and rest in our natural state. Otherwise, happiness, like love, may get projected onto others, and we miss the opportunity to directly experience our heart essence. Lasting happiness will then elude us.

The dissatisfaction we feel when our search for happiness in relationship fails is actually a gift. It can point us to the true source of lasting happiness. We don't really want to settle for fleeting, inconsistent experiences of happiness. We all want lasting happiness. We simply need to acknowledge that happiness is inconsistent in relationship. Sometimes we are happy with our partner and sometimes we are not. This can change from day to day and moment to moment. If we are open and pay attention, we will hear the message in this inconsistency: *We are looking for lasting love and happiness in the wrong place.* It cannot be found in these changing circumstances. Our discontent is telling us to look for a deeper, permanent source of Love within.

When we look in the right place, we find an abiding happiness and peace of mind in the aware presence underlying all experience, whether it appears positive, negative, or neutral. This happiness and sense of wellbeing is here, no matter how we are feeling about our partner. To recognize and relax into this presence is to discover that it contains all the happiness we could ever want, an endless supply delivered fresh each moment. Once we begin falling in love with the source of happiness itself, we discover an unconditional sense of well-being that pervades all experience, whether it is the high of falling in love, or the low of losing a loved one. When we fall in love with an ever-present contentment, our life energy and attention can then flow toward the source of Love, while still fully appreciating and enjoying our relating with others. The more we come to know the source, the less separate we feel, and the more our capacity for intimacy and Love grows.

Knowing this truth can radically change the way we are in relationship for the better. In my own experience, I feel less and less affected by the ups and downs of the relationship with my husband. This is due to the ever-deepening realization that he is not the source of my happiness. When you know that happiness and well-being are an inside job, it sets you free to accept your partner exactly as they are. There is no need to control or hold on to them. You know that happiness is not lost when relationship challenges arise, so there is no need to push them away. We discover that happiness can be found in the midst of the challenges. It may be impossible for the rational mind to understand this, but *our happiness is not dependent on any person or circumstance.* The underlying, true happiness is here, whether or not we are in a relationship, and whether or not there are challenges. It changes everything for us to know this. Rupert Spira (2013) shares, "The discovery that peace, happiness, and Love are ever-present within our own Being, and completely available at every moment of experience, under all conditions, is the most important discovery that anyone can make."

The Biology of Falling in Love

Not only is the experience of falling in love a glimpse of our essential nature, it is also a temporary biological experience that is mediated by the biochemical processes coursing through our human brain and nervous system, which gets confused and labeled as "love." This biology has a purpose; nature designed humans to bond and mate. We are designed to be sexually attracted to each other so we will propagate. We are also designed to bond and support each other in the care and protection of children.

Much research has been done on the neurochemistry of falling in love. Helen Fisher, research professor and author of the seminal book, *Why We Love: The Nature and Chemistry of Romantic Love* (2005), focused her research on dopamine, norepinephrine, and serotonin. All three of these neurotransmitters produce many of the sensations of human romantic passion. Elevated levels of dopamine and norepinephrine in the brain produce many of the characteristics of romantic love, such as extremely focused attention and exhilaration, as well as many of the other feelings that lovers report, including increased energy, hyperactivity, sleeplessness, loss of appetite, a pounding heart, and more. There may also be impaired judgment and blind acceptance of our beloved, which may have influenced Chaucer's declaration that, "love is blind." Decreased levels of serotonin are associated with obsessive thinking, and have been found in people experiencing the first flush of love when they can think of nothing other than their beloved. It is no wonder that the ancient Greeks called falling in love "the madness of the gods!"

The interaction of these and other biochemicals provides a very real and potentially addictive experience. Some people believe that being in love is nothing more than this biological experience that occurs for the purpose of procreation and child rearing. Yet Love can't be entirely explained with science. The truest Love is a vast mystery that includes, but can't be limited to, biochemistry or an emotional experience. All human forms of love occur within Undivided Love, which includes and transcends biochemistry and emotion.

The opportunity to recognize a greater Love most often gets lost in the swirling flows of powerful neurotransmitters, hormones, and emotions. The all-powerful Love of our true nature is a subtle and quiet presence that can be drowned out by the strong currents of our emotional and physical responses to being in love. It takes awareness, commitment, and discernment to recognize what is lasting and most true in the compelling experience of falling in love. Yet this is well worth the commitment and attention. It can lead to the most profound and beneficial discovery possible for a human being—an infinite and indestructible Love that will enhance relationships immeasurably and sustain them over time. Discovering Undivided Love is the best thing anyone can do to improve, heal, and sustain relationships. Recognizing the source of Love keeps our relationships alive and fresh.

I would like to share how knowing the source of Love can radically change and enhance the human experience of falling in love. Lucia's story is an example of how awakening to this understanding brought an inner stability, clarity, and compassion that transformed her experience of falling in love.

Practicing Awakened Relating

Lucia: Staying Awake in the Dream of Romantic Love

To put Lucia's story of falling in love in a meaningful context, I will first share the story of her awakening. When I first began working with her in therapy, Lucia had never been involved with a spiritual practice and would not have described herself as a seeker. Yet, I could feel a deep openness. I found myself compelled to speak of awakening to a deeper truth, even though she did not initially appear to be interested in this. Lucia later reported that she had no idea what I was talking about, but she could feel it resonate as true.

A sudden and profound awakening to her most essential nature occurred at a time of crisis when Lucia was feeling lost and confused about who she was and where her life was going. One day, while she was sitting at home with her head in her hands feeling a deeper despair than she had ever experienced in her life, she thought, "This is not who I really am. This misery, and all the thoughts and feelings that go along with it, is not who I really am." Lucia saw that she had a choice to stay in that despairing state and identify with it or not. Then, she prayed sincerely with all her heart to be taken beyond this mistaken identity. She said, "In that moment, I gave everything up. I let go. I surrendered. Then I felt at peace. At that point, I saw that I was not what I had always believed myself to be all my life."

The change was sudden and dramatic, but it lasted, which is rare. For most people, the awakening process is usually more gradual with many experiences of "getting it and losing it." Lucia reports that, "The recognition of my true nature has remained. My old self is still here, but it is not at all who I am. I am all that I thought I was, and everything else, yet beyond it all at the same time. This changed my life completely, and I am very humbled by it."

Lucia's shift in self-identity has been challenged in many ways since that breakthrough moment. Now, the focus is on embodying that realization in relationship and all areas of her life. Not long after this opening, Lucia experienced falling in love and found it to be radically different than ever before. "When I fell in love in the past, it would just pull me under completely. All my attention and focus would be dedicated to that. There was no clarity because it was clouded by the mental projections and emotional dependency of being in love without awareness of the source of the Love. It was all projected onto the partner." Since recognizing her true nature, Lucia reports that even though she has strong feelings for her partner, she also feels a powerful love for herself, the world, and all of life. In the beginning of the relationship, Lucia remembers telling her partner, Rachael, "I am actually in love with everything and everyone, and you are a part of that." Her consciousness and attention did not narrow down to a focus on one person, and instead she saw Love as the essence of everything.

There was an emotional experience of "being in love" occurring, but it was part of the whole of life. In Lucia's words, "There was a human emotional experience that was different, but not separate from infinite source. I just knew clearly what the source of Love was. The deeper sense inside of me, that greater Self in me, that was the source. And, I felt that source in everything. Love was everything."

Knowing herself as the source of Love allowed Lucia to have a much freer and more relaxed experience of being in Love without grasping at it. This allowed her to take her time with the new relationship. Ordinarily, when people are in love, they jump in with both feet and spend every possible minute together. Yet, Lucia did not have the urgency of her prior experiences. There was no rush. She was able to spend time easing into the new relationship, allowing it to move in a natural flow.

Lucia describes her new way of being in relationship: "Knowing the source of Love allowed me to accept things about my partner that I would not have been able to accept in the past. There were so many things that the old Lucia would never have been able to accept. Rachael's addiction was one of the big ones. Yet, now I just let life happen, without needing it to change in any way. I know that I cannot control life. I can only accept all of it as it is. So, when things come up with Rachael, I just address it directly and clearly in the moment, without holding on to any particular outcome. I made it clear to her in a very loving but firm way that she was free to continue her addiction, but I would not be a part of that. There was not even a trace of trying to manipulate her in that. I was just standing in my truth, from a place of freedom and clarity with a strong boundary. There was no judgment. It was like, 'I am not going to make you change,' but rather, 'I want to make it clear where my boundaries are.' I felt detached and unconcerned about what her response would be. It was completely okay either way. I love her, but if she chose to continue the addiction, I knew I would be able to leave. I could never have done that in the past. Never."

Knowing that she is not dependent on any one person for Love and security gives Lucia the freedom to be with everything that arises in relationship. She has nothing to lose because she knows she will not lose the infinite source of Love, security, and well-being. Lucia knows from the depth of her Being that Love can never be lost. Therefore, she could be at ease with the whole process of falling in love and starting a new relationship. She says, "I operate from a different place now—from a place of knowing that absolutely everything is okay. I can't forget that deeper knowing now. It is always here no matter what comes up. All is okay exactly as it is."

MEDITATIVE INQUIRY:
Finding the Love Within

I invite you to do a brief inquiry into the source of Love. Take a few minutes to just relax. Relax the body and the mind into the underlying awareness, or on the movement of the breath. Take your time to gently settle into the present moment.

Now, intentionally think about someone you love—a lover, a child, a pet—any being you love now or have loved in the past. Notice the warm feelings in your heart that they evoke. Notice that this experience was evoked *within* you. The loving feeling did not come *from* them. They only appeared in your imagination and that appearance triggered an experience of Love or warmth. Both the feeling and the image arose within the field of your awareness.

I invite you to let go of the image of the one who evoked this loving feeling within you and be open to whatever experience of true Love is present in your heart. See if you can sense that a deeper Love is within you, independent of any image or emotion, but not separate from them. True Love may take the form of a soft compassion, a subtle peace, or a quiet stillness. This Love is not limited to the emotional, human version of love we are familiar with.

You can also contemplate what is evoked by these words from Eckhart Tolle (2003):

Feel the essence of Love within you, inseparable from who you are, your true nature. The outer form is a temporary reflection of what you are within, in your essence. That is why Love can never leave you, although all outer forms will.

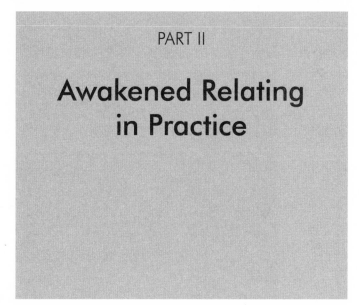

PART II

Awakened Relating
in Practice

CHAPTER 5

The Challenged Heart
Relational Wounding

No matter how difficult the past, you can always begin again today.

—Jack Kornfield

Once the fairy dust of falling in love settles, we are left with the inevitable challenges of intimate relationship. This does not need to be a problem. In fact, it is the gift of relationship. There is an immense potential for healing and awakening in relationship struggles. Surprisingly, the most beneficial gifts are found in our greatest challenges if we are open to receiving them. When met with love, clarity, and openness, these challenges are doorways to greater freedom and deeper relational harmony.

Relationship challenges can seem far away when we are first in love, but they are often lurking in the background, ready to emerge. We may have fallen in love with a person's heart essence, but their ego structure is made of conditioning and often relational wounding. Our partner's conditioning inevitably collides and clashes with our own. Eventually, we discover that our partner cannot be the all-encompassing source of happiness we hoped they would be. We start to see their imperfections and inconsistencies in loving us. We begin to judge them and come into conflict over our differences and the ways we disagree.

Intimate relationship also brings up our own unmet emotional needs and we discover that our partner cannot fulfill all these needs. Romantic love makes a seductive promise that all our unfulfilled needs

from childhood will now be met. This is probably the most disappoint-
ing illusion of the romantic dream. Also, relationship has the potential
to bring us to the realization that our partner cannot satisfy our
deepest longing for union with our own Being. Every human being has
this longing, even if we are not conscious of it. These disappointments
can drive the wedge of separation deeper into a relationship, dividing
it into painful fragments. Or, we can learn to cooperate with the
deepest potential of these failures, which involves returning us to our
shared Being. As John Welwood says (2006), "Our pain at the hands
of others forces us to go deeper in search of the true source of love."

However, no matter how awake we are to our true nature, we still
have our emotional and psychological "stuff" to deal with. We have all
been conditioned into separation and duality, which creates psychological disturbance in varying degrees for everyone. It does not all
magically disappear once we awaken to the source of Love. We must
address the challenges on the mental and emotional levels of our
human relating. We cannot fully solve these problems at the level on
which they were created, but they can be transformed in awakened
consciousness if we allow ourselves to fully experience them. Otherwise,
we can cycle endlessly in variations of our conditioning and wounding,
never being free of it.

We can only *fully* meet and allow our emotional and psychological
issues in the unconditional compassion and acceptance of awakened
consciousness. The ego "me" will continue to resist anything that is
uncomfortable, preventing it from being released. The unconditional
allowing of our true nature is what has the power to resolve our pain
and wounding. As Adyashanti (1999) says, "We need to meet the
'stuff' from our awakened consciousness. Then and only then can it be
truly released and transformed. You are not looking from it, but at it
from a place of clarity, wisdom, and compassion." This is far too simple
for the conditioned mind to understand, so we often miss it!

Without knowing this simple truth, we can spend many painful
years struggling to improve ourselves and our relationships through
books, couples counseling, workshops, meditation, and so on. Although
improvements can and do occur through these efforts, they are limited.

If we don't consciously include and rely upon the unlimited intelligence of Being, our efforts cannot fully transform these issues and we may even miss the underlying freedom and harmony that has always been present.

Releasing Conditioning in Undivided Love

In my clinical and personal experience, the issues which most interfere with relational harmony arise from our conditioning that has shaped our sense of a separate self and our perception of the world. We see the world through a prism of our conditioning. Some of it is positive and some of it is negative, but we are all subjected to it. As babies, we learn what works and what doesn't work to get our parents' attention and to have our needs met. In the beginning of life, we mainly form our sense of self through what we see in the eyes of our caretakers. Through the responses and actions of others, we develop our sense of self. We are all conditioned to perceive and experience relationship in particular ways. Our parents or primary caretakers are our models for relating and we learn how to be in relationship through observing them and absorbing how they interact with us and with each other. Some of those models are positive, but most of us had less-than-adequate modeling for healthy relationships.

Our conditioning only becomes problematic when we identify with it and believe it is real and true. Conditioning is just thoughts and associated sensations and feelings floating in the space of aware Being. Freedom and healing occur as a result of becoming aware of the patterns these thoughts create and eventually awakening out of them. Working with conditioning is always part of my work as a therapist. First, we need to become conscious of how conditioning shapes our experience of our self and the world. Then, we need to see it for what it is—beliefs and learned patterns that we took to be true and made into an identity. Such limiting ideas are never the truth of who we are, but until we see this clearly in the light of awareness, we continue to play out our conditioning unconsciously.

Awakened relating is the true transformer of our conditioned mind. Psychotherapeutic approaches are most skillfully used when they are informed by the wisdom of our unconditioned nature. Then, we are tapping into an infinite intelligence that is the most potent force for transforming our suffering. Using healing modalities to shift an illusory separate identity can be helpful, but it will not free us from the fundamental misunderstanding at the core of that illusion. As we wake up from this misunderstanding, we can begin to relax our conditioned experience into its source. This allows conditioned patterns to be released because they are all made of the universal source energy that everything is made of. The patterns dissolve back into this source when they are fully allowed. When we offer no resistance, they arise from that source, appear for a while, and naturally return back to it. This is both the simplest and most powerful of all solutions. Conditioned patterns naturally release when not resisted.

Cracks in the Foundation: Relational Wounding

It is very common for conditioning to include relational wounding or trauma, which disturbs our ability to have healthy intimacy in relationships. Trauma therapist and author Laurel Parnell (2013), defines relational trauma as "trauma that occurs in the context of relationship— either something that happened or did not happen (e.g., neglect) to a person that has caused him or her harm." Given that definition, we have all experienced relational trauma or wounding to some degree. Addressing this wounding and exploring how it can be finally resolved is essential in developing an ability to be in healthy relationship. In Chapters 5 and 6, I will discuss how awakened relating can transform our relational wounding.

Relational wounding or trauma may result from unhealthy treatment by any family member or in other significant relationships, but most importantly from the relationship with our primary caretakers. We are most susceptible to relational wounding in the early years of our lives when we are so vulnerable and we still relate openly in an undefended way. This open innocence is closer to the undefended Love of our true nature. But, as children, all too often we have been hurt in our vulnerability and learned to build defensive structures in order to protect ourselves. These are the imprints that shape our later relational life. Because we are so impressionable as young children, the conditioning becomes deeply imprinted in our nervous system and psyche.

When we become adults, and want to engage in the openhearted relating that we all long for, our conditioning arises and sets off a danger signal in the nervous system that it is not safe for us to remain open. At this point, it is important to bring the light of compassion to these hurt parts of us and not make ourselves wrong for this. As children, we protected ourselves the best way we knew how. Now, we can learn to open our hearts again in the safe haven of our deeper nature.

There is a wide range of relational trauma and wounding. The more severe forms of relational trauma in childhood include: physical, sexual, and/or emotional abuse, physical or emotional neglect or abandonment, early loss of a parent or primary caretaker, a parent's mental or physical illness, and drug or alcohol abuse. Many common experiences that are not considered traumatic can also result in relational wounding. A parent who is chronically unavailable emotionally for any reason causes relational disturbance, and so does a parent who is overly emotionally involved and invasive. Having a parent who is consistently controlling or critical also disturbs our sense of self and therefore our ability to relate. Another significant source of relational wounding is lack of mirroring and attunement. If the parent does not mirror the goodness of the child with their eyes, facial expressions, voice, and touch, or doesn't attend to the feelings and needs of the child, the development of healthy bonding and self-esteem is disturbed.

The conditioning that results from these early relational disruptions makes it more difficult to navigate all the ups and downs of intimate relationship. These early stressors can limit our capacity for intimacy and make us more easily triggered in relationship. I have worked with couples that are walking through a minefield of triggers with each other at all times. The more awakened awareness we have, the more possible it is to navigate these challenges.

Resolving Relational Wounding in the Unshakable Ground

How can this relational wounding be truly resolved? No matter how many cracks we may have in our conditioned foundation, we *always* have the solid foundation of the ground of Being, which is the root source of our healing. The primordial ground is within all beings, even if we haven't yet consciously accessed it. Our unshakable foundation was never touched by trauma, or any relational disturbance. No amount of pain or fragility can prevent you from recognizing who you truly are. The loving, kind presence of our essential nature is silently waiting to be discovered at the core of all our deepest wounds and hurts so it can soothe and heal them.

Awakened awareness, or Undivided Love, is the most powerful, alchemical solvent. It has the power to dissolve or resolve anything in its presence, even serious relational wounding. Lucia, whose story of awakening and falling in love was told in the previous chapter, is an inspiring example of being present with the serious relational trauma of childhood sexual abuse. Before her awakening, she was not aware of the rage, terror, and grief associated with her trauma. She was shut down, rarely allowed herself to cry, and never felt anger. Her relationship with Rachel was the catalyst that brought these feelings up to be met and released. Lucia's awakening was sudden and dramatic, but the integration and embodiment of that has been a gradual and challenging process that is primarily taking place in relationship.

Lucia beautifully describes her commitment to being with the pain of her relational trauma: "For a couple years now, I've made feeling pain a sacred and consistent practice. I set time aside to be with the most difficult, terrifying, and heart-wrenching pain I have ever let myself be with by doing the most courageous thing I can think of: *I feel it.* As I remain detached from my mind's stories about the emotions and sensations, I focus on releasing them from my body while remaining aware of the presence of Being. I own every piece of it." This courageous practice has allowed Lucia to release and transform these energies, which has created more space for Love and healthier relating with Rachel, as well as more resting in Being. (See the Appendix for Lucia's story of releasing a deep fear that was a symptom of her trauma through the power of awakened awareness alone.)

The Sensitive Heart: Insecure Attachment

Relational wounding, particularly in the first few years of life, can result in an insecure attachment to our primary caretakers. This creates a bond that is lacking in trust, safety, nurturing, and consistency. The child feels as though they are on shaky ground relationally. Our early attachment patterns determine how well we function in relationship later in life. Early attachment and bonding is an extremely important aspect of human development. In the field of psychology, secure attachment is the foundation of a healthy psychological and relational life. Old wounds from childhood in the areas of bonding and attachment will inevitably be reactivated in close relationships later in life. However, we can become conscious of our insecure attachment patterns and learn how to bond in healthier ways.

We develop an insecure attachment when our caretakers are neglectful, engulfing, inconsistent, or abusive. When our innate drive to connect is met with an inconsistent response, an overwhelming response, an absence of response, or a dangerous response, an insecure attachment is formed. In this way, we don't learn to feel safe or at ease in ourselves or in relationship. On the other hand, we will develop a secure attachment when the caretakers are available and loving enough to give us a basic sense of safety and security, which then carries forward into all our relationships for the rest of our lives.

Fortunately, if we did not have a secure attachment in childhood, it can be "earned" or developed later in life. When this is earned, secure attachment includes the ever-present ground of Being, and we gain an even deeper sense of safety and security that is much more solid and real. This has the power to free us from the pain of trying to find safety and security in another person who is also struggling. Once the secure ground is found within, it provides a solid foundation for relating that cannot be shaken. We may distract from it, but whenever we turn to it, it is here. All else comes and goes within our ever-changing experience. Our fundamental nature is the one and only presence that will never abandon us. How could it? It is what we are!

My client Phoebe's experience is an example of the transformative power of the ultimate secure base of the ground of Being. The healing of her relational wounding involved recognizing, resting as, and relying on her deeper stable nature, as well as on being present with her pain in a shared field of awakened awareness with me. Phoebe beautifully describes how it has been for her since finding this secure base: "I've got it within me now. I found it within myself. All is well. No matter what happens, deep down I know that all is well. This is all the Love I was always looking for. I have found the Beloved. I am being loved and nurtured from within at all times now. I know that I never leave home. This knowing is a soothing nectar that is calming my nervous system." When this understanding appears to get lost, Phoebe reminds herself of this truth and is now able to return to it either quickly or over time with support. (See the Appendix for Phoebe's full story about healing her relational trauma.)

To stay present and awake with our conditioning, relational wounding, or insecure attachment patterns that arise in relationship, we may first need assistance with being present with these patterns within ourselves. Sometimes people need to practice this with the support of a therapist or others for some time before they can succeed in staying awake in the midst of wounding being triggered in intimate relationships. It can be vitally important to get support. The reactions that come from relational wounding and trauma can be so strong and compelling, it may, at first, seem impossible to just allow them to be without lashing out at others or turning on ourselves.

In my experience, developing an earned secure attachment most often requires a focus on three levels: relationship, body, and true nature. This involves a safe, healing relationship (whether it is with a therapist, an intimate partner, or someone else), skillful, therapeutic work in the body that addresses the imbalances in the nervous system created by early attachment wounding and/or trauma, and awakening to the secure ground of Being.

My therapeutic work with both Phoebe and Deborah demonstrates how powerful it is to work on all these levels with relational trauma. For Deborah, a secure attachment was first experienced in a therapeutic relationship, which then carried over to her personal relationships. For others, this can happen within their intimate partnership, or with a friendship. It was Deborah's struggle with relationships, both with herself and with others, that brought her to therapy. For more than twenty-five years of working as a psychotherapist, I have found that the most common reason all clients seek therapy is relationship challenges.

Practicing Awakened Relating

Deborah: Dissolving the Barriers to Relating

The beginning of Deborah's life was marked by abandonment. Her birth mother gave her up for adoption and her adoptive mother was not able to provide a secure attachment or a safe environment due to her own unresolved relational trauma. For a while, Deborah's only safety was with her adoptive father, until he betrayed her by molesting her when she was an adolescent. These ruptures resulted in relational trauma, which made it difficult for Deborah to have healthy relationships. She didn't know how to really let people in and feared being abandoned. Deborah did not trust others and never felt safe in close relationships.

Deborah is committed to her spiritual process and was eventually able to recognize the awareness that is her basic nature, rest as that, and rely on it to meet this wounding. At first, Deborah was more comfortable resting as awareness within herself with eyes closed. She was learning to trust her natural state within herself, but was not yet able to be that while connecting with me. Relationally, I could feel a barrier between us that became increasingly subtle over time, but it was there. I was not truly allowed in.

Eventually, when we tried meditating together while gazing with open eyes, Deborah's attachment issues showed up right away. The first issue to show up was lack of trust. Deborah saw that she did not trust that I would not abandon her. As we began resting in the field of awareness together, she sensed the barrier between us, which she was not previously aware of. At one point, Deborah said, "I am not going to let you in unless you can promise me that you will never, ever, ever leave!" It was clear to me that this demand was coming from the hurt child within.

Without doing anything other than staying with this experience within the field of shared awareness together, she spontaneously dropped down into the body and into her heart. This opened into enough relational safety to allow the contact to be received. I could feel this shift within my own body. Suddenly, I was let in. Now, there was a beautiful energetic flow between us that felt deeply nourishing to both of us. With tears in her eyes Deborah said, "This is what I have always wanted! I've always wanted this my whole life—to have someone be fully present with me and feel safe and connected."

For Deborah, there was a dramatic shift when she came into relationship with me while resting in undivided awareness and remaining aware in the body. She reports, "The difference was night and day. There was a 180-degree shift. I had a certain level of trust built up from the therapy we did before that, but not in a way that was going to allow my nervous system to relax enough to really take in relationship. That was not going to happen without the safety of this greater awareness. It just wasn't going to happen. When I am relating entirely from the conditioned mind without the safety of awakened awareness, it is difficult, if not impossible, to break down the barriers and develop the trust and safety needed to heal my wounds. That's just not possible. But, as we sat together in the field of awareness, the barriers just dissolved naturally, or they were seen and not attached to or identified with. When those old patterns came up in this open space, they could be allowed here.

For me, it was about dropping out of the conditioned mind and into underlying awareness, which created a sense of safety in relationship that I had never known before. When I am not identified with my conditioned mind, I am not anxious. I am not anxiously attached. That was a very important experience for me to have. From that deeper level of safety, it was possible for me to explore being in direct relationship with you without my protective barriers, and to fully allow whatever discomfort came up. It is okay to allow myself to be in relationship when I am resting as awareness and the nervous system is relaxed. This was a new experience for me.

In one of our sessions, I clearly saw how every bit of my conditioning and conditioned identity could fall away completely, if I just hung out in Being long enough. That's really all that is needed. All conditioning can just fall away and then, no one is a threat."

MEDITATIVE INQUIRY:
Being Present with Relational Wounding

I invite you to be with a trigger that comes up frequently for you in relationship. It would be best to start with a reaction that is not too highly charged—about a four on a scale of one to ten. Sit with this reaction when it occurs, or think about the last time it occurred.

Be willing to just sit with the trigger without analyzing it or thinking about it. Drop the story and feel into your body. What do you notice? Be aware of sensations and feelings such as constriction, tension, anxiousness, numbness, sadness, or anger.

If the feelings or sensations are strong, notice what places in the body feel okay, such as the bottom of your feet or the tips of your fingers.

It is important to focus on what feels good or neutral. If you can't find anything in the body that is at least neutral, find something in your environment that feels soothing to look at and feel into that. This supports the nervous system in being with a charged experience. You may also want to ask someone to sit with you while you are being with the reaction. If it feels safe, they can offer supportive touch.

Now, if you can, be aware of the underlying ground of awareness that is noticing it all. This awareness is holding all your experience in a welcoming openness. It can simultaneously be aware of itself and all pleasant, unpleasant, and neutral sensations.

Allow whatever you are experiencing within the embrace of the larger acceptance of your Being. This is true Love meeting all the reactive, wounded parts of us that long to be soothed and resolved. Rest here. Let Love touch all these places with the tender caress of unconditional acceptance.

CHAPTER 6

Mending the Wounded Heart

Healing With Awakened Relating

The distance from your pain, your unattended wounds, is the distance from your partner. And the distance from your partner is your distance from the living truth, your own great nature.

—Stephen and Ondrea Levine

Awakened relating is the most powerful healing force available for mending a wounded heart. Most of our emotional and psychological wounding occurred in relationship and therefore must be healed in relationship. A relationship that is grounded in awakened Love has the most potential for this healing. All our relational wounding will arise within our closest relationships and awakened relating makes it possible to allow that to unfold and transform in a deep embrace of Undivided Love. This provides the courage and wisdom to meet the enormous challenge of facing our relational wounds that arise in relationship while remaining awake to our deeper nature. As Adyashanti (2004) says, "To remain as you are, which is simply the light of awakeness, in the midst of relationship is the most challenging thing that a human being can do." Yet this is how we heal our wounds and awaken our consciousness.

The higher purpose of relationship is to awaken consciousness. It is more fundamental than having companionship, sharing pleasure or happiness, or having a family. If we align with this higher purpose, intimate partnership supports our awakening and evolution, individually and as a species. As Eckhart Tolle (1999) says, "If you accept that relationship is here to make you conscious instead of happy, then you will be aligning yourself with the higher consciousness that wants to be born into this world." If we are open and willing to become more awake in our relating, it is a much happier experience. Awakened relating opens us to sharing the inexhaustible happiness of our unlimited Being, which is the true "happily ever after" for each of us.

Relationship is a catalyst for awakening consciousness by making us aware of the obstacles that obscure the true reality that shines beyond and through our conditioning. It is important to know that our relationship struggles can point us back to our natural state of harmony and ease. If we perceive the challenges as something to be avoided or gotten rid of, we fail to notice their message, which is: *Look deeper and see what is already free and whole.*

The Gift of Inner Radar

One of the ways that infinite intelligence assists us in our healing and awakening is to provide us with an "inner radar" that attracts the right partners with which to work out our wounding and who will support awakening our consciousness. This radar is largely unconscious. On a conscious level, we seek out those whose conditioning agrees with our conditioning, in a misguided attempt to connect. Yet even if we find the conditioning agrees in some ways, it will inevitably conflict in other ways. The true meeting that we all long for can never be found in the conditioned identity alone. We can only find true intimacy in the unifying field of pure awareness beyond all conditioning.

We will naturally attract intimate partners who fit a certain amount of the conditioning we received from one or both of our parents. Most of us do not realize that our relationships mirror our own unconscious conditioning. We typically attract partners at a similar level of psychological and emotional maturity who are similar in some ways to one or both parents. This creates relational patterns that repeat an aspect of our family conditioning. For example, if we spent our childhood trying to please an overly critical parent, we may attract a partner who is also critical and continue attempting to please them while not standing up for ourselves. At the same time, we may remind the critical partner of their mother with whom they are angry for not standing up for herself, which makes them more critical. The playing out of our conditioning in relationship is uncomfortable, but it is a gift. It provides both partners the opportunity to recognize and let go of these patterns, enabling them to relate in a new way and potentially discover the already present harmony and ease.

In the beginning of a relationship, we mostly experience the positive aspects of the parental conditioning that our partner evokes. Later, our partner will evoke the more painful conditioning. Their behavior may eventually elicit some of the negative feelings we had with our parents, such as helplessness, shame, insecurity, and rage, among others. We unconsciously attract what is familiar, even if it is not at all what we consciously want. I have witnessed many people carefully try to select partners as different from their family as possible on dating websites, and still end up attracted to someone who is a match for their unconscious conditioning. It may appear to be different at first, but it eventually shows up. We can't really fool our inner radar!

Although it is an important first step, simply becoming aware of our conditioning will not fully resolve it. Until we awaken our consciousness and allow unconscious patterns to resolve in wakeful presence, they will rule our perceptions and choices. The purpose of our inner radar is to create relationships that will allow this resolution to occur. Rather than resisting relationships that activate the tender, hurt places within us, we can welcome these uncomfortable experiences in the compassion and wisdom of Undivided Love. It is important to note, however, that working with relational wounding is best done with a partner who is self-aware and willing to take responsibility for their conditioning.

This welcoming requires an unwavering commitment to what is most true in the moment when our wounds are touched. Otherwise, we get swept away in either our reactivity or denial. Although for most of us this may seem impossible at first, we just do the best we can, one moment at a time. We will now explore how to be with charged triggers while in relationship.

Relaxing into the "Hot Spots"

Each relationship has what I call "hot spots" that are very charged and difficult to relax with. Hot spots are where a couple's conditioning related to their relational wounding and traumas collide. These are the times when both partners are triggered and neither one may be available for awakened relating. These painful hot spots are the most challenging and potentially explosive situations in intimate relationships. As I have mentioned, this happens frequently, since we tend to attract relationships where our mutual wounding gets recreated. We somehow manage to find the right person to push our "hot buttons" so they can finally be healed. As Adyashanti (2004) warns, "Anything that is unmet or unseen will be like a little button with a 'push me' sticker on it—and it attract fingers."

At the beginning of our relationship, which began in 1991, my husband John and I did not yet have direct recognition of our essential nature. However, we had a conscious relationship. We were aware of many of our conditioned patterns and projections, and to the best of our ability, we took responsibility for them. But, when our relational hot spots flared, we did not yet know how to rest in and rely on pure awareness. Even after recognizing our essential nature, it took a while to begin embodying that in our relationship.

This came about over time through our main practice of repeatedly giving attention to the presence of awareness in our daily lives. As we continue to notice and relax into the wakefulness that is always there, it becomes a stronger, more consistent and stable presence, which we have come to rely upon in our relationship. It has been a gradual process for both of us. I will share an example of one hot spot that we have relaxed into overtime, which is John's defensiveness colliding with my need to be heard.

To create the context for our hot spot, John and I both had alcoholic fathers and codependent mothers, which resulted in relational wounding in each of us. John's father was physically abusive and critical. Through this experience, John learned to get very defensive when he feels criticized or blamed in any way. My father was mostly absent from the family, drinking away from home. I spent much of my childhood pointing out that this was a problem, which was met with denial by my mother. Since my reality was not validated in this and many other ways, I developed a need to point out what I perceived as "wrong" in hopes of being heard.

My need to be heard triggered John's hot button around being criticized. And his tendency to defend himself triggered my hot button of not having my insight validated. These hot spots can cause powerful reactivity, which can only be *fully* allowed when we consciously notice the detached, awake space in which they are arising. Otherwise, we will either defend against these experiences or get caught up in them.

The challenge was to stop and allow the strong currents of energy that this trigger stimulated in me to move through my body-mind without projecting it onto John, or acting it out in some other way. Sometimes it took all my commitment to do this, and, even so, there was a high failure rate in the beginning! The reactions would just take me. I could go from "zero-to-sixty" in a few seconds, and so could John. The biggest challenge of being in a hot spot together is that neither partner may be available in the moment to remind the other of what is most important and true. Yet, John and I began to relax into the underlying awareness whenever we remembered to do so, whether it was during or after the reaction. Over time, we experienced resolving the hot spots, slowly in some cases, and quickly in others. With core wounding, we need to rest repeatedly in the midst of these reactions over time before they finally dissolve and resolve.

From John's perspective: "In my experience, as we have each retrained our attention to focus more on the clear, open presence of awareness, rather than our conditioned points of view, Lynn Marie and I are both becoming freer to allow our conditioned patterns to arise and allow their living energies to move through our Being, while still experiencing and expressing the kindness and Love that radiates from the nature of our Being. I am finding that as my moment to moment resting with whatever is occurring gets more frequent and lasts longer, I am much quicker to drop my fixed, defensive stance, and I am able to be in the vulnerable openness that lies beneath it. Then, I can pause, disarmed, not yet knowing, and wait for a response from my unguarded Self. As I relax into this, the neurochemistry of my upset settles and I am, once again, available and loving."

Healing Insecure Attachment with Awakened Relating

Our attachment wounds are relational and therefore require relational healing. It is awakened relating, a combination of awakening and relationship, which is the key to transforming these ruptures. Awakened relating provides the context of safety, security, love, and wisdom, which offers us what was not available in childhood. This safe container allows these wounds to be faced, experienced, and released.

The two most common forms of insecure attachment are referred to as "anxious" and "avoidant." A person with an anxious attachment will be hyper-focused on relationship and anxious about any separation or perceived abandonment. A person with an avoidant attachment will be the opposite; very independent and needing a lot of space. As you might expect, these two patterns often attract each other in intimate partnerships, and they can drive each other crazy until these issues are met with understanding and awareness. Even without an insecure attachment, the pattern of one partner being a pursuer and the other being a distancer is a common way that intimacy problems manifest in relationship.

April: Healing Insecure Attachment in the Ultimate Security

April and her partner Ryan are a classic example of an anxious/ avoidant combination. She developed an anxious attachment because of inconsistent attention from her mother. Sometimes her mother was very present with April and enjoyed engaging with her, but then she would suddenly become depressed and be minimally available for extended periods of time. The inconsistencies in the bonding and attachment process caused April to become anxious about loss of connection, not knowing when it was going to happen next.

Her partner, Ryan, on the other hand, had a mother whose attention was mostly absent, rather than inconsistent. She was always preoccupied with something—television, reading, hobbies, smoking cigarettes—while ignoring Ryan. When he approached her wanting contact, he usually heard, "Not now." Therefore, Ryan developed an avoidant attachment and learned to devalue his need for relationship. He became independent, believing it was better to just be on his own and not need others.

For April, it was a recipe for suffering to try and resolve her early life issues of aloneness and abandonment by wanting more connection with a partner whose wounding causes him to be uncomfortable with connection and want more distance. The more she turned toward Ryan to give her what she felt was absent or lacking within herself, the more he pulled back energetically, emotionally, and physically. The more he pulled back, the more anxious she became. Since there was no resolution to be found in this distancer/pursuer pattern, it drove April to look for a deeper solution.

Awakened relating provides a secure base to rest in and rely on as these patterns arise. It is the one solution that allows us to be present with the pain of these attachment ruptures, revealing a deeper safety and security that the partner cannot provide. Then, clinging to our partner or avoiding our partner are not our only options.

With commitment and perseverance, April is healing her core attachment wound through awakened relating. She has a life-long commitment to psychological growth and spiritual awakening. As April's recognition of her true nature deepened, she became more aware of the contractions and reactions that emerge in relationship with Ryan, and she has been more able to be present with them.

Relational disharmony has become the doorway or the stimulus for April to notice, rest, and allow what is arising in awakened consciousness. As April says, "The more I am resting as awareness, and meeting everything and everyone including Ryan and myself *as is*, the distinction of a 'me and other' diminishes, and the reaction reveals itself as none other than true nature. This is a huge relief, to say the least, in intimate relating! The more I rest and allow relational patterns and habits to be met with the openness of simply allowing them to be, the sting of the separate self softens and is seen as an expression of my basic nature."

When we begin to release our long-held patterns of attachment, feelings such as fear, loneliness, shame, and anger may arise. The challenge is to stay present with them rather than reach for our partner. For April, a deep aloneness came up when Ryan distanced himself from her. When she was unable to be with the despairing aloneness, she was compelled to reach out to him to remedy that. April reports, "My tendency was to go there, rather than stay *here*. As I reside more and more as the awareness I am, the compulsion to reach out naturally shifted to reaching in. Or, more accurately, I allowed the external grasping and then noticed it fading away. This hasn't been easy, but it is far more free and loving."

This shift has been an outcome of April's resting and relying on awareness moment by moment. The more she experiences her essential core in the midst of anxiety or any strong disturbing affect, the greater the inner stability she experiences and the less need she has for soothing from outside. As she says, "I feel deeply committed and devoted to being with what is, as it is. I have discovered that I either do short moments of resting as true nature, or I experience long moments of suffering!"

As we learn to take responsibility for our attachment patterns and rely on an ultimate secure base for healing, it opens the relationship up to more love, compassion, and gratitude. Without the grasping and avoiding, both partners are free to love each other as they are and come to know an Undivided Love that does not abandon us, ever.

Practicing Awakened Relating

Isaac and Meike: Holding Each Other in the Tender Places

I was interested in interviewing my friends Isaac and Meike because of their deep commitment to awakening and bringing it into their relationship. They are committed to being present with all the conditioned patterns that arise in relationship, including both the subtle and raw and painful patterns. This is not only their commitment with each other, but with all of life. They both consider themselves to be "an invitation to what we all know and to uncovering all the automatic unconscious patterns that confuse us." They hold meetings around the world inviting others to share in what they are committed to living.

Isaac: If we take a look at what relationship is, it breaks down to a bunch of spoken and unspoken agreements, promises, and commitments. We can look and see if we keep the agreements we make with ourselves. These days, the marriage vows are, "I will stay married in sickness and in health, in good times and in bad, until death do us part … or until I change my mind." When we look at the agreements that are made, spoken or unspoken, they are all about trying to avoid pain.

It seems to me that we just don't know what life is going to ask of us. We just don't know how it is going to play out at any point. We really don't have a clue. We have a Hollywood version of relating, but that is not how it really plays out most of the time. There is so much conditioning around relating—what's okay, what's not. I see how the tendency of the mind wants to always make relationship into something, to put it into a container. In fact, relationship is a mental construct. Relating is all there is.

Most of us are confused around hurt. We have all experienced hurt in relationship, but few of us have examined how it happens. We make agreements to try and control each other so we won't feel hurt, but that doesn't work. What I notice in how relating happens for Meike and myself, and how we have developed over the years, is that there is very little projecting in terms of blaming each other for upsets that happen. Most commonly, there is an asking to be met in whatever comes up. Usually when there is an upset that is about the other person, there is no blaming the other or our self.

Most of the wounding people have is about our parents having the habit of a dualistic focus and seeing us as objects. Therefore, they were not able to truly feel or see us and then misread our signals. Since our survival depended on them, this felt existentially threatening and so our nervous system did not develop in a healthy way. Our nervous system needs information from another nervous system to be able to feel that everything is okay and that our needs will be met. When this need to be felt, seen, and appreciated is not met in early life, it shows up as a yearning that often gets entangled with the idea of being loved. Fortunately, our systems can receive the information they need later in life, but not if the idea of being loved remains unexamined.

There is a need for being felt, seen, and appreciated, and for the quality of attention that we can call love. Our sense of self is relational. We don't exist in a vacuum. As pure awareness, there are no wants and needs, but to the tissue of the human body there is. What I have noticed is that when difficult dynamics come up with Meike and me, like when she went through menopause or when I have emotional pain, it can take everything to just be present with it all. It is not always easy to be kind and gentle and to meet in Love with experience like that. But, it makes such an enormous difference.

Meike: Our relating has been, and continues to be, a journey. I would say that we have come a long way. Our shared interest in Truth as our priority is a great grace and has assisted us in our relating. We place that first, above relating. It has always been that way. With that, we can always come back to our deepest knowing. Whenever our conditioned nervous systems automatically go into projection or separation, or see the other as the source of Love, we have been blessed to know of the truth beyond that. Our life is based on that.

So far, we have been experiencing a continuous falling into the unknown. We always come back to presence, to ask, "Is this actually true?" Now our nervous systems can hold conditioning and patterns that I wasn't even aware were there—all the deepest, deepest wounding and everything dark that you can imagine. We are slowly being able to gently be present and hold each other's hands in that. It takes everything, the totality of who we are, to be embodied and present with our deepest wounding.

In the beginning of our relating, upsets would happen, but we would have opposite patterns in reaction to the upset. My system would pull away, while Isaac's system would push for connection. It took us awhile to notice what was going on. If we didn't see it, our nervous systems would get terribly upset with each other. We saw that if we went with that, we would end up in a hell. At first, we began with just noticing what was happening and understanding that we would regret it later if we went with it. So, we would take a time out. We didn't disconnect, but we separated for a while to let our bodies and nervous systems calm down and then came back together again. There were sometimes huge upsets in our systems.

Over time, our systems learned a new way of being with each other. Slowly, we became friends in upsets instead of enemies. Now, we are both able to hold the conditioning of our nervous system without blame. If something shows up in consciousness that normally would throw us into a felt sense of separation, our nervous systems are now able to stay present with that. If it is too much, we go into time out, but most of the time we can hold hands through most of what comes up. And, sometimes it seems endless actually. It is amazing what comes up!

Isaac: If we are living from the perspective of separation, the quality of attention that is given is actually painful. It could be called abusive relating. When you are living in a dynamic of abusive relating, how can you invite something different? It starts out with a lot of love, then you touch the wounding and the nervous system goes into fight, flight, or freeze. If this is not resolved, that kind of relating is going on all the time, which is actually a form of violence.

Meike: The moment an upset arises in the body, it comes with a strong sense of "I," which always will be perceived as separation. When that is noticed, I can now reach out, even if there is an upset. There can be all the sensations of separateness, but when it is noticed as that, we can reach out and invite gentleness and a felt sense of connection with the so-called other.

Isaac: An example is that Meike would disappear for two or three days sometimes. At some points during these times, I would see her and let her know that I can see something has been touched in her. I would tell her, "I am your friend, and I am your beloved. If I can, I would like to meet you here." There was a time when I did not know quite how to deal with a partner being upset. I would usually try to change or fix it. When you try to fix or change it in any way, it makes it worse. It's really about just being present in it from a vulnerable place. It is not about coming from, "I have it together and you don't, so I will help you." It is about being vulnerable and available. We are both learning to be available to each other when things are touched. Now, it is really easy in a way. I can see that everything that happens builds more trust. It brings about a feeling that she is really here for me.

For men, when a woman is upset, it can touch old wounding from their mother, especially when the upset is projected onto the guy. It can be very terrifying. But, I try to meet her there anyway, because there is a knowing that it is not personal to us and it doesn't mean anything. There is recognition that it is not personal and it is an opportunity that will benefit both of us, and all of humanity.

Meike: We have come to recognize how our nervous systems have been wired or conditioned from the beginning of life and have slowly learned to be gentle with that. Sometimes it is very, very difficult. There are blind spots where we don't have any knowing. There are collapses in my nervous system that happened as early as in my mother's womb that I didn't know about for a long time. We can hold each other in these nervous system organizations that were traumatized so long ago. And, sometimes there is deep upset for no reason. It can just be how our cells perceive things.

LML: How do you sit with these early patterns in the body? Do you simply allow them to be as they are?

Meike: Even less than that. Just the pure seeing of it is enough. Adding any effort at all is too much. Now, it is very clear that noticing is enough, and then resourcing myself. I resource whenever possible through doing things that are comforting for me. What I do to resource depends on how deeply my system has been touched and how much it goes automatically into disassociation. I would give the system simple orientation, such as feeling my feet on the ground or looking around to allow the body to find itself in time and space. I would let the body check to see if its environment is safe. Sometimes my favorite smell or just going for a walk would assist to calm the body. Sometimes I would ask a friend to hold me in their arms. There is no need to dive into the painful experience, noticing is enough, and then resourcing whenever possible. This is how my nervous system is being educated and finally releasing the traumas it holds.

LML: Simply being present and noticing is like having the fragile parts of us held and soothed by the presence of awareness.

Meike: Yes, the presence of awareness is the embodied mother. She is holding everything without any effort. The baby doesn't have to do anything except grow in the warmth of the mother's loving eyes and embrace.

MEDITATIVE INQUIRY:
Being with "Hot Buttons" Together

I invite you to practice reaching out to your partner (or a friend) when they trigger one of your relational "hot buttons." Providing they feel safe enough, and are not triggered themselves, you can ask them to support you in being with the reaction. Instead of lashing out, or holding back, you can try asking, "Can you sit with me while I allow myself to just be with the intensity of this reaction?" They don't have to do anything. They can just sit and be present with you, hold your hand, or offer a touch on your back or shoulder, whatever is supportive and non-intrusive. They can also remind you to rest in the deeper relief that is always here in whatever is temporarily moving through.

This is taking full responsibility for your hot buttons, knowing truly it is not about the other person. Courage and humility are needed to respond in this way. This can also feel very vulnerable. The ego-self only wants to move away, into or against the reaction. But, our true identity has infinite space for allowing the reaction to unfold in its loving presence. This is most healing when it occurs relationally in loving support.

With this support, just allow the charge to move through your body-mind while you continue to relax into the present moment, dropping down out of the head and out of any story about what is happening. Feel the sensations and emotions directly in the body, until the clarity and presence of Being opens up again naturally. Then you can respond to your partner (or friend) with Love and wisdom, if you feel moved to do so.

CHAPTER 7

The Undivided Heart
Awakened Conflict Resolution

Knowing one's true nature does not mean that there are no conflicts.
But it does change how one approaches them.

—Rupert Spira

Awakened relating is not about being in a continuous flow of blissful harmony and never having any conflict. Conflict is part of human interaction. Since we are each uniquely different, conflict is inevitable. It is important to let go of our concepts of what awakened relating is supposed to look like so we can discover how it expresses itself. It can look like anything and everything, as long as the source of the relating is grounded in Undivided Love. We may even get angry and raise our voice at our partner from a place of pure Love and find it is perfectly what was needed in the moment and caused no harm. All ideas of perfection are just ideas. What is most important is where our relating is arising from within us. Is it a movement of Undivided Love or a movement of our divisive, reactive mind?

It may not make sense to the dualistic mind, but it is possible for there to be a deeper, continuous flow of harmony amid conflict, or anything else that arises in relationship. The underlying continuity of the unconditioned presence is not dependent on eliminating conflict or anything else. This harmonious flow, or Love, is the substratum of all experience and its presence can be consciously known no matter what is occurring. If we make it our priority to emphasize this substratum, we will find that conflicts resolve in beautiful and sometimes surprising ways. When we choose to rely on and trust the harmonious flow that is Love, then we access an infinite intelligence that is always available to provide solutions to all apparent problems or conflicts. This conscious emphasis on the substratum of Love is not passive. On the contrary, it means that we are taking responsibility for what is arising within and between us, which is an essential element of awakened relating and conflict resolution as we awaken together into the fullness of our uniqueness within our shared field of oneness.

Taking Responsibility

When we prioritize staying awake, this allows us to take one hundred percent of the responsibility for our part in any conflict or disharmony that arises in relationship. Even if we perceive that our part is only one percent, we take one hundred percent of the responsibility for that one percent. We take the focus off our partner and put it only on our part of the conflict. No matter how small it may be, we always play a part in any relational discord. Most couples I have worked with begin therapy with pointing the finger of blame at the other. The first step is to assist them in turning their attention toward themselves—not with self-blame, but with a sense of responsibility. Both people are equally responsible for keeping an unhealthy relational dynamic going.

Since one person usually appears to be the "problem" and the other the "victim," I will use this extreme, hypothetical example to illustrate how each person is equally responsible for any unhealthy dynamic. One person may come home in a rage and physically or emotionally harm their partner. This person can appear to be the entire problem, and the other person an innocent victim. However, the "victim" can learn to take responsibility for the low self-esteem or believed powerlessness that led them to be in an abusive relationship. If we look honestly, we can see our responsibility in any situation. It is always there. One person being the problem is never true, no matter how much it may look that way to the dualistic mind. Taking responsibility takes us out of that mind-world of projected blame and victimhood, releasing us into the living, undefended, and openhearted experience of awakened relating.

For my husband John and me, it has required a deep commitment over time to sit with burning impulses to react with blame or attack and not act that out. It is important that we give up our "right" to be a victim of our conditioning. Whether we learned to be a victim or a victimizer, we can take responsibility for this conditioning. Taking responsibility is made more possible as we wake up to the indestructible stability of Being and come into balance within our body-mind. Along with the initial awakening to our true nature, this willingness to take responsibility is a necessary step in awakened relating.

Once we start flexing the responsibility muscle and begin turning the finger back toward our self, it ignites a trajectory that takes us to resolution and freedom. We can see in our own experience how painful it is to point outward, and how it creates more feelings of separation. Taking responsibility frees up massive amounts of energy that are tied up in blame and projection. Then, that energy can flow and open into more love, harmony, and connection.

Yet, even though our experience tells us it is freeing to take responsibility and it is painful not to, it is often difficult for us to actually do it. The ego-identity does not want to direct attention back to our self and notice that we have been choosing, even unconsciously, to participate in painful relational dynamics. To do this loosens the stronghold our ego-self has had on us, which is initially difficult if we have been strongly identified with it. The less identified we are with the ego-self, the easier it is to take responsibility for our actions.

Most conflict arises because of not taking responsibility for our part in whatever is occurring. The divided self likes to make others, or anything outside itself, wrong, rather than looking at itself. Awakened relating requires that we have the courage and honesty to look at our self and see what is not working and where we are stuck in unresolved aspects of our conditioning or wounding. If we are truly honest, we can see that what is causing us to be in conflict with another is really about parts of us we have not yet accepted or healed that are being projected on our partner. They may have triggered our wounding, but that is within us. Our partner is not responsible for our feelings, nor are we responsible for their feelings. Our feelings result from our mind's conditioned interpretation of what is occurring.

Whenever we find ourselves in conflict, it is an opportunity to look in the mirror and see what is being reflected back to us. It's always about how things are being mirrored back to us, and how each relating is showing us another version of our wounded and false sense of self. This is the gift of conflict. It shows us where our separate identity is holding on the most. As we come into harmonious awakened relating, more of the Love and beauty of our true Self is mirrored back to us. As Eckhart Tolle (1999) says:

> Every conflict and crisis in a relationship is an opportunity for more growth, more awakening. If we resist or deny these opportunities, then we miss the gift contained within them. … Instead of mirroring to each other your pain and your unconsciousness, instead of satisfying your mutual addictive ego needs, you will reflect back to each other the love that you feel deep within, the love that comes with the realization of your oneness with all that is.

As we become willing to take responsibility for our thoughts, feelings, and actions, it is important to know *how* to do that. Whenever we are presented with a conflict of any kind in relationship, we have several options. We can go with our reaction to it, we can deny it, or we can remain present with it. I would like to explore these options in a way that will allow you to see for yourself that we only have one true option that works, which is to allow everything to be as it is within awakened consciousness. From that, we find resolution to all conflict, which is always created through some form of resistance to what is. Once we understand that resistance is the root of all conflict in relationships, we only need to relax our resistance into our unconditionally accepting nature. This is the one solution for all conflict. This does not mean giving in. On the contrary, it means choosing to stand in what we recognize to be the deepest truth and dealing with issues from that clarity.

The Only True Option

The Buddha taught that the source of suffering is the attachment to desire or craving, which includes both desire to have (indulge) and desire not to have (avoid). We continue to suffer by responding to our experience with either indulging it or avoiding it. Both of these responses prevent us from being present with the experience in the moment. When we are challenged in close relationship, or in any moment of life, these are the only two options available to the ego structure of our apparent separate self. This self is nothing more than a simple defense mechanism that has a very limited repertoire of responses. The healthier an ego structure is, the subtler and more flexible our responses are. The more unresolved wounding we still have, the stronger and more rigid our reactions will be. Either way, some version of indulging and avoiding is all the ego-self has to offer when faced with conflict in relationship.

When we avoid or indulge the pain that arises from our relational wounding, we are preventing its healing. To truly resolve or transform our pain, it must be fully met and directly experienced within the open space of innate awareness. Avoiding and indulging are ways we move away from direct experience. If we avoid direct contact with our pain, we also lose direct contact with our deeper nature, which is where the resolution or dissolution of our suffering can occur. These defensive responses also create separation and distance from our partner, which results in more conflict. If we are not connected to our own, living experience, we can't be genuinely connected with others. The deep irony is that we are trying to protect ourselves with our defensive responses to life, yet they are what creates our suffering, prevents our healing, and keeps us feeling separate from those with whom we long to feel closest.

To evolve beyond these deeply ingrained impulses, we must fully understand and face the truth that they keep us imprisoned in separation and suffering. We will not let go of them and be willing to meet our pain directly without clearly seeing we have no other true alternative. Therefore, let's inquire into each of the impulses to avoid or indulge and see where they take us.

To indulge in what arises in relationship, or within ourselves, means to react to, buy into, act out, engage in, cling to, lash out, and create stories—in other words, to get lost in our responses and reactions. We tend to indulge thoughts, feelings, sensations, desires, states of mind, and relationships while forgetting the context in which every experience is occurring. The best option is not to ignore or try to stop any experience; it is simply about *including* the underlying ground.

Look closely and honestly at your own life and see if any type of indulging has ever resolved an issue in relationship. You can also look and see whether indulging is creating additional problems as well. I invite you to pay close attention to this in your relationships and see clearly what happens as a result of indulging.

To avoid whatever arises in relationship means to deny, reject, ignore, push away, repress, distract from, numb out, bypass, evade, withdraw, shut down, or disassociate. We all have tendencies towards either predominately indulging or predominately avoiding our experience, depending on our personality, the situation, and our conditioning. In my marriage, I have primarily been the indulger and John has primarily been the avoider. This is a common combination with couples. But we all do both. And both are forms of resistance to *what is*.

Look closely at your own experience and see whether avoiding your experience resolves your issues or pain. Does it appear to work temporarily and create bigger problems in the long run? Can you find a time when this was not true in your life? Has avoiding issues in relationship ever resolved them? I invite you to reflect on this honestly and see for yourself.

Our only true option is to allow everything to be as it is while maintaining direct contact with our unconditionally accepting nature. We will not be able to allow everything to be as it is without knowing and emphasizing the stable basis of all experience. This is key—recognizing and prioritizing our true nature is what makes it possible for us to be free in our experience and not enslaved by avoidance and indulgence.

If we do not have access to our deeper nature in any moment, it does not mean that we can't allow our experience to simply *be*. You can always relax the mind out of the story and feel into your heart or belly while allowing feelings and sensations to move through. Focus on the breath. The breath is always immediately present and noticing it can serve as an inner source of calm and stability. Also, paying attention to whatever else feels positive or neutral in the body, such as the hands and feet, will support you in being present with uncomfortable feelings and sensations. As I discussed in Chapter 5, with deeper wounding or trauma, it is important to get whatever support you need in order to fully be present with these challenging experiences.

At best, we can only temporarily neutralize our experience through avoiding or indulging. The limited options of the ego-self are truly impotent in the face of relational conflict and wounding. These strategies move us away from conscious presence and out of awakened relating. They cause us to try to squeeze the living moment into the preconceived notions of our conditioned mind. Instead, we can choose to refocus our attention and open into alert presence with willingness and wonder. When we make this choice, it returns us to the source of all real solutions to our relational problems. All other solutions are partial and temporary at best, and harmful to others and our self at worst.

The following conversations share a mature couple's experience with awakened conflict resolution. Rupert and Ellen are a married couple, but I interviewed them separately for this book. They each share their experience with meeting conflict from an awakened understanding and the larger context of undivided awareness. Their experience shows that conflict, which can otherwise cause so much painful separation, offers deeper awakening and connection when it is met with love, compassion, and clarity. As we open fully to our most difficult conflicts in relationship, they reveal the greatest potential for healing, freedom, and intimacy.

Practicing Awakened Relating

Rupert: Resolving Conflict in True Intimacy

In the following conversation with Rupert, a nondual spiritual teacher, he speaks of being with conflict within the context of the true intimacy of our shared Being. This involves knowing that the conflict is arising from each of our conditioned identities. When we are viewing the conflict from this knowing, we do not try to resolve it on the level of our conditioning and we clearly see that the resolution or dissolution of the conflict happens in a meeting of true intimacy.

Rupert: Knowing one's true nature does not mean that there are no conflicts. But it does change how one approaches them. If both parties know that their essential nature is unconditioned awareness, then it is clear that these conflicts are occurring between what is conditioned in each of them. It is a "clash of planets," so to speak. What both parties *essentially* are cannot be in conflict. And the resolution of conflicts is not in working out the conditioned problems, although there is, of course, a place for exploring conditioned problems. Problems are truly solved by accessing that within us that is inherently free of conflict. That is the "placeless" place of true intimacy and the source of resolution. If each party stands knowingly as that, any further conversation about the conditioned aspects of the conflict stands the best possible chance of reaching a resolution in an intelligent, efficient, and loving way.

The place where all problems are resolved is in true intimacy, which means the loss of boundaries and the loss of that which defines us and makes it seem like we are something that is temporary and limited.

If one is in a relationship where both parties know how to meet in true intimacy, then that is the source of continual renewal in the friendship. It is a renewal that does not exclude conflicts, but puts them in context. There will nearly always be some amount of conflict on the level of form because forms are separate; they are not merged. On that level, there will always be issues of some sort to explore and work with. But, if those issues are worked out in the context of true intimacy and we know that meeting in intimacy is the way conflicts are really resolved (or dissolved), then that is the source or wellspring of the relationship. In this way, the relationship is not a battle between two conditioned forms or egos trying to derive happiness from each other. The secret of relationship and the source of its freshness and renewal is to know where to find intimacy—not in the object and not in the other.

LML: Can you give an example of how this understanding would appear in relationship when a conflict arises?

Rupert: For instance, if you are in a conflict with your intimate partner, the conflict is always a clash of conditioning, a clash of conditioned thoughts and feelings, which, by definition, are conditioned because they have form. Any conflict can only be between two different forms of conditioning. The first thing is to know for oneself that what one *truly* is, is not a conditioned object, a limited mind and body. If we truly know that we are this unconditioned awareness, then we know that for the other. If that is what I essentially am, then it must be true for all apparent selves.

To know that what one essentially is behind (though it's not really behind) this screen of conditioning is this unconditioned openness. And, to know that the other is this as well, takes the personal sting out of the conflict. It doesn't mean that there may not be something to resolve on a relative level, but you don't necessarily look for the resolution of the conflict on that level. You know that if you want true resolution, you both need to step out of your conditioned point of view. You need to step out of the boxing ring where two points of view are fighting each other. To step out of that (though you don't really step out of that) is to know who you truly are, for the other to know who they truly are, and to meet outside the conflict. Then, *that* has an impact on the issue being discussed.

This doesn't mean the conflict magically goes away. There may be something that needs to be discussed, but you no longer do it as a separate self that is seeking happiness from the other. In other words, you bring true Love and true intelligence to bear on the situation. That gives the conflict the best possible opportunity of being resolved in a way that will restore harmony to the relationship.

Ellen: The Gift of Conflict

Rupert's wife, Ellen, is a psychotherapist and a teacher of authentic movement and yoga. She shared her experience of how awakened, nondual understanding influences her experience of being with conflict in relationship. Nondual understanding involves knowing the fundamental unity that connects us all and underlies all experience. Whether this understanding appears to be temporarily lost or not, it is always returned to and is the focus of Ellen's devotion. She sees conflict as a gift in that it continually points us back to what is most true and reveals all the ways we hide from this truth.

Ellen: You can understand at the level of the mind that objects do not bring happiness, they appear in happiness, which is our nature, but as my teacher Francis Lucille used to say, "Relationships are graduate studies." They push our understanding to a much deeper level. You either know your true nature or you don't, but being established in that is another thing. That takes time. But, it really doesn't matter how long it takes when we are no longer focused on the relationship and we are focused on the truth.

LML: The truth becomes the first priority as we realize that the relationship can't be the source of Love and happiness.

Ellen: Although sometimes it merges with the source, it becomes the first face of the source. At other times, it becomes the first face of our ignorance!

LML: Can you share your personal experience of being with conflict in relationship from an awakened perspective?

Ellen: In my experience, there are moments within conflict that are unenlightened and just heated. This is when one of us is expressive and reactive—usually me—and the other is the polar opposite, usually Rupert. We are polar opposites, and that constellates whatever baggage we brought to the relationship, sometimes in a very acute way. In those moments, it seems like the light has left the relationship entirely. And, in a way, it has. In a way, we are at the mercy of a kind of energy, a kind of force. There is no clear seeing in those moments.

Then, there comes a time, whether it is a few minutes or hours, when you gain some perspective. You start to see more clearly and the emotions abate. You sometimes need to take some space. Then, the understanding comes back into the foreground. In my case, it is as if there are moments when I lose this understanding that the truth is what I am really going for and instead I am scrambling to get what I need or I am defending myself. There is a full deployment of the separate self. Then, the awakened perspective returns and everything calms down. I take space to really be with the feelings and bring clarity to the situation and try as best I can in that moment to turn back toward presence. When the presence comes back into the foreground, then qualities such as empathy, openness, and a desire to come together again in the understanding arise. This happens effortlessly.

In my experience, I don't apply the nondual understanding to the relationship. It arises naturally because I am deeply in love with my true nature and I have chosen a partner who is also. Conflict appears as a gift in the nondual understanding. It's the yoga of this understanding. I can't imagine not having these big waves of energy because they excavate all the hiding places that haven't yet been revealed. These places are not revealed when you are on your own or when life is comfortable. Only being in an intimate relationship can do that. Nothing else can do that.

LML: This is true. Relationship is the passport when we want to come out of all our hiding places. Nothing will strip our egos naked like relationship does when it is held in the crucible of our shared oneness.

Ellen: Yes, and sometimes having our ego stripped naked is not what we want, because it can be so intense! Isn't it? Sometimes I run away from it with everything I've got. At the same time, there is such a deep desire for the truth and I have come to trust that, when conflict is in service to the truth, it will be fine. Conflict does not have to be a trap when it is in service to deeper awakening. Then, we are not using it just to perpetuate the separate entity.

LML: It depends on what we are committed to in any given moment. When we come back to clarity when caught in conflict it is because that is our commitment. We want to remain in alignment with our understanding more than we want to defend our ego or be right.

Ellen: Yes, if there is a longing to align the actual shape of the relationship with our peaceful, open nature, we return to that again and again. There really is no solution to be found in the separate entity. It is just a complicated web of fear, desire, patterns, and habitual reactions.

LML: None of that offers a real solution to our conflict and suffering.

Ellen: No, not at all! I want to emphasize that life is so intelligent. Even the moments when we might project on our partner, say something very hurtful, raise our voice, or withdraw, are gifts for our partner.

LML: Then we are offered the opportunity to either get lost in our reactions or to allow those uncomfortable thoughts and feelings within the clarity of awakened understanding.

Ellen: Sometimes the awakened understanding is not enough. In other words, we may also need psychotherapy processes that can help us learn what to do. It can be like, "Here I am caught in a reaction with my partner, but I never saw a model of how to be with this in a healthy way." You might be able to be with the openness and presence of awareness, but not yet have the tools or skills to know how to relate in a healthy way. This is where I feel the nondual psychotherapy explorations that people such as you are offering are very helpful.

LML: For many, both awakening and therapeutic exploration is needed. If we only do psychotherapy without nondual understanding, then the therapy is limited. And, if we only go to nondual awareness and are lacking relational skills or have unresolved wounding, it will limit our capacity for awakened relating.

Ellen: Some people may have the deeper understanding, but it might not be sufficient to remind the body of its true nature of transparency and limitlessness. So, you do some exercises that help to expand the body in this way and are given tools that help us with this. I believe that in relationship we need tools very badly! Most of us were not given these tools by our parents. And, our spiritual teachers are not necessarily giving us those tools either. That is not what spiritual teachers are there for.

Relationships will call up a lot of layers that were dormant. True intimacy would be to meet in this openness, and, then, as the layers of fear and vulnerabilities appear, we share them openly together. We stay in that openness and welcome whatever comes. Each partner can help the other to do this.

LML: There will be times when one gets lost and the other doesn't, so they can help. There will be other times when both people get lost. That is the most challenging. But, we keep coming back. It doesn't matter who does that first.

Ellen: Relationship is a little bit like meditation on your own when you are abiding as this presence and all of a sudden, a resistance comes up. This is an invitation to inquire into who is this "me" coming up and appearing as something other than this presence? Relationship is the same. When there isn't conflict or reaction, relationship can be a celebration of the presence. What a beautiful thing it is to share presence. A relationship offers so many ways to express this—sexually, intellectually, and emotionally. Sometimes I feel so inept at relationship. But, that has nothing to do with nondual understanding. When I let that idea go, I see that I am simply grappling with it all and that's okay.

LML: Exactly! I don't think there is anyone who has the nondual understanding perfectly embodied in intimate relationship, at least no one who I know of. It's perfect that you are grappling with it—so am I. We are all grappling with it at this point in our evolution.

Ellen: I hope that people who read this book will feel that it is such a relief when the relationship itself is relieved of having to provide Love. I remember once early on in our relationship when I was really struggling with Rupert and wanting something from him and being needy. He spoke to me forcefully, and said in no uncertain terms, "Ellen, don't go for the relationship, go for the truth!" It came as if it was the voice of God. It was a shock to the little separate entity, but it really cut through to the truth. Then, there was such a relief in that understanding. Nothing was being taken away at all. There is an infinite abundance of Love.

LML: That is a beautiful example of how we can help each other stay awake in relationship.

Ellen: The other thing that has been helpful between the two of us is to say something about the other in its raw, unedited, naked truth. Not to throw it at them, but to say it directly as a fact. For example, saying something like, "You are unsupportive." To just say your truth as it is, or to hear it from the other as it is, that's the gift of living as this openness. It cleanses or opens up a space that makes it safe to speak to one another.

LML: It is safe when we do not fully believe a relative truth such as, "You are not supportive." It is being allowed within the absolute truth that is its ground. The tricky part is fully allowing it without losing the larger context.

Ellen: Yes, the tricky part is when we lose the openness and we are defending. But, as soon as you open, it is amazing how you are at home, even when something is uncomfortable and difficult to say or hear. When the openness is in the foreground it can be remarkably easy.

LML: Without the openness of our true nature, we cannot allow anything without getting caught up in it. It's impossible.

Ellen: No. It is just not possible. The true resolution is found only in the true intimacy of meeting in the vast openness of our shared Being. We can't ever know what that will look like, but it will always be a movement in the right direction towards more Love and intimacy—that's the only way it can go.

MEDITATIVE INQUIRY:
Taking One Hundred Percent Responsibility

Pay attention to times when you blame your partner for a conflict that arises in relationship. Turn the finger of blame into self-responsibility by pointing it back on yourself. Even if it is small, there is a part you played. Notice what aspect of your consciousness participated in creating the conflict. Was it unresolved relational wounding? Was it holding onto a belief? Was it projection of an unwanted part of yourself onto your partner? Was it an unconscious unmet need? Often, the source of our part in a conflict is unconscious. This can require a deeper contemplation. Our feelings, bodily sensations, and relational patterns are clues to what is held in the unconscious. So, it is important to be present with them.

If there is resistance to looking at yourself and taking responsibility, be present with the manifestations of that—contractions in the body, feelings, and fixed thoughts and stories. All of this experience gives us a strong sense of a separate self in opposition to what is. Notice the awareness in which all of this is occurring, including your sense of self, and allow the whole thing to be as it is. In this way, conflict gives us an opportunity to awaken out of the conditioning that creates conflict and the creator of conflict—the separate self.

CHAPTER 8

Telling It Like It Is
Awakened Communication

If we really want to communicate, we have to give up knowing what to do. When we come in with our agendas, they only block us from seeing the person in front of us.

—Pema Chödrön

Awakening to the truth of who we are will not automatically give us good communication skills. That is something we all have to learn. Since most of us did not learn these skills in our families, in school, or through the media, we need to find ways to learn how to communicate in our relationships. I had to learn communication skills for myself before I could teach them to my clients. However, we may still find it difficult to tell each other the truth even after learning these skills. If we are operating entirely out of our conditioned identity, we will only be able to communicate its needs, its agendas, its interpretations, and its projections. In other words, we will only be telling the truth from our egocentric perspective. Awakened communication ultimately involves dropping all the ideas and agendas of the conditioned mind and resting in a field of open intelligence, which will then reveal what is most true in the moment.

Telling the Truth

Telling the truth is about being with things as they truly *are*, rather than how we believe they are, or what we think about them. We can't possibly see the truth of *what is* when we are looking through the filters of our concepts, beliefs, labels, and descriptions. Through these filters of the conditioned mind, we are only communicating our mind's inter- pretation of our experience and the person, which is always limited and never the whole truth. No matter how skillfully we do this, it will not produce any true communication. Therefore, it will not result in any lasting connection or resolution.

Many of us learned that telling the truth meant downloading our conditioned mind and spewing out everything we think about people, literally giving them a "piece of our mind." However, this is not telling the truth in the way I am pointing to here. To begin to access what is most true, we need to let go of our points of view (or at least hold them lightly) and sense what is true in the silence within our body and Being. As we are fully present with our experience in the moment, we can get a felt sense of what is truly authentic. This may be a sensation in the body, such as a knot in the stomach, a deeper feeling or emotion, the silent presence of our Being, or all the above. We could say that these are different layers of what is true in the moment. The deepest truth is always the absolute truth of Being, and there is also the rela- tive truth of our human experience. They are not separate. *Awakened communication is the willingness to tell the truth on the deepest level we have access to in any given moment.*

It can take time to sit with feelings before we can communicate them honestly and authentically. For example, we may be aware of feeling angry, but if we are present with that in the open field of aware- ness for a while before we speak, it may reveal a deeper truth. Angry feelings toward others are often a defense against feeling the vulnera- bility of what is truer, such as, "I'm hurt," "I feel insecure," or "I feel alone." If we don't sit with it first, we might angrily say something like, "I am so angry that you are not there for me while I am going through this!" When what is true is, "I am scared and I need your support." If we communicate the most authentic truth we know, it leads to more connection, and the other person can hear us more easily. When we communicate defensively, it leads to more conflict and less connec- tion, which is not what we want or need in relationship. Most importantly, our defensive responses keep us out of direct contact with the deepest truth underlying all experience.

Telling the truth may feel frightening to our sense of a separate self. Honesty requires letting go of the ego's agendas to feel safe, to seek security, and to be accepted by others. It may feel scary to let those agendas go and trust a deeper, truer source of safety and security because it is unfamiliar. It takes courage to tell the truth. However, the more we access the true source of well-being, the less we feel a need to defend and protect our self, or to seek safety and love in others. We might still do that for a while out of a deeply engrained habit, but we no longer need to.

It also takes humility to tell the truth. The ego "me" is always trying to put its best face forward and avoids exposing any imagined imperfection at all costs. It takes humility to tell the truth about all the insecure, frightened, self-centered, manipulative, and judgmental parts of our personality and conditioned identity. Yet, we come into unity within ourselves and within relationship through a radical honesty that fully allows our humanness within the context of our vast nature. This humility arises out of direct knowing of who we truly are and a growing dis-identification with our conditioned identity. If we know that false identity is not who we are, then we feel it is okay to tell the truth about what it is expressing.

One of my main focuses when working with couples is to help them find and speak their truth to each other. There can be such a wide chasm between them if they have not told each other the truth for a long time. According to Deepak Chopra (2006), "Ninety-five percent of the problems in relationships exist because of lapses in communication." Sometimes all that is needed to heal the relationship is to speak honestly, even when it is hard to hear. We all have reasons for why we don't tell the truth. We may be concerned about what others will think of us, we may fear rejection or abandonment, or we may fear being harmed in some way.

The defensive responses only work temporarily, at best, and they never really protect us from anything. In fact, they will eventually lead to the very thing we are trying to protect ourselves from! We try to protect ourselves from rejection or abandonment by not telling the truth, and we usually end up rejected or abandoned because the withholding creates distance and loss of connection. We try to protect ourselves from being judged by not telling the truth, and we end up being judged because we are not being authentic. If we are in a relationship where we are being harmed emotionally or physically, not telling ourselves the truth about what keeps us in an abusive situation allows it to continue. It is always wise to tell ourselves the truth. When we rely on the clarity of our innate intelligence, it will guide us in knowing when and how to tell the truth to others. In addition, good communication skills will also help us tell the truth in a way that is beneficial to all concerned.

Listening with an Undivided Heart

When we are listening to others, we are usually focused on our interpretations of what they are saying. In other words, we are only hearing what we *think* they are saying. We may not even be able to hear them at all above the noise of our own mental narrative. Or, we may be anxious for them to stop talking so we can respond impulsively from our reactions. This is not what I would call awakened listening.

Imagine listening without paying attention to the commentator in our head. Imagine listening with a vast, open receptivity. It means listening from our openness and being receptive to what the other is saying as well as our own responses. This is being open to it all without holding on to anything. We would then be an undivided space of openness receiving the other person and their communication *as it is*, rather than through the filters of our mind. This is awakened listening.

When we are listening with an undivided heart, we do not take anything that is said personally. We are not just listening from within our personal self that we need to defend or protect. We know that whatever is being said can never harm the indestructible presence that we are. It is safe to accept what is being said, even if we find it difficult for the "me" to hear. It is important to remember that whatever anyone says about you is far more about his or her conditioning than it is about you; it is their projection. However, if we can receive whatever is being communicated without resistance, we are more likely to open up to the Love that is always present and the wisdom to know how to respond in a loving and clear way.

Making it Safe to Tell the Truth

We need to feel safe to tell the truth, especially in intimate relationships where we are most vulnerable. The deepest possible safety is found through *being* Being. Our own Being is already free of all reactions that occur in communication, but not separate from them. By being that, we naturally meet only the truth of the moment, not our interpretation of it through the mind's filters. It is simply safe to be with *what is*. But, if we rely on our divided sense of self, it has nothing to offer other than avoiding our feelings and reactions or indulging them; neither brings any real safety.

I would like to share experiences of awakened communication from couples that are trying in their own ways to speak and live the deepest truth they know in relationship. Their examples demonstrate the living experience of learning to rest as and rely on the safety of Undivided Love. This has made it safe for them to be honest and authentic with each other. It also provides the wisdom to know when to communicate and when to allow our experience to unfold within our own Being. It's important to remember that this is not about doing it perfectly. Perfection is only a concept in the mind. Remember that we are all pioneers with awakened relating. It's best to explore this new frontier with wonder, creativity, joy, and patience.

Simon and Isabelle: Harmonious and Respectful Communication

Simon and Isabelle are deeply committed to practicing awakened relating. Here they discuss how communication has developed for them since they made this commitment and discovered ways to communicate consciously and respectfully. Their main practice is resting or relaxing into shared Being. They rely on this to guide them as to how or when to communicate their feelings and reactions in relationship. They have found this to be a deeper solution than relying on their old patterns of communication or on methods and techniques. They recognized, however, that if communication tools arise when they are relaxing in Being, they are always appropriate and much more effective. (See the full interview in the Appendix.)

Isabelle: In the beginning of our relationship, we used old, unsuccessful methods of communication, which made relating challenging. We were quite motivated to find a way that worked. We really wanted to find the right way to communicate harmoniously. That intention has really had a profound effect. We now know how to speak to each other in the most harmonious way, and this just grows and grows. We are learning how to communicate consciously and are learning how to address each other respectfully. For example, I will say, "I have this idea about what we should do now. How is that for you? Is that okay with you?" We always find the most respectful way to communicate with each other and with our children. I highly value that.

Simon: One of my old communication patterns was to always be defensive and expect criticism and blame from my partner. At first, I expected this from Isabelle and when she did not blame me, there was empty space. I didn't know what to do with that! I was out of my comfort zone. It was an adjustment to be with that. It was fascinating and a bit scary at the same time because it wasn't familiar.

Isabelle: We both wanted a new way of communication without the shame and blame game, but we were so used to expecting a certain response from the other that it took a while to learn to relax with that. It was the relaxation in Being that helped us move beyond this. We would see the pattern and relax with it, and then a more harmonious way of communicating started to emerge naturally. At first, it took a while for us to find our way to clarity again. Now, it happens quickly and easily.

Simon: We also don't dump our emotional garbage on each other. Most of the time, we stay with whatever reactions we are having within our self and take responsibility for it. Sometimes we might need to take a little time out and withdraw for a while and relax within our self. That is seldom, but if I feel overwhelmed, I will withdraw and take time to relax within myself. Then, we meet again and the communication is clear. Sometimes things come up and we take responsibility for them and never say anything at all to the other. In my case, it could be frustration or a sense of lack in something. I can experience feeling closed off, or many other experiences within myself. Isabelle can sense that, but it is not always necessary to share it with her. She knows and trusts that I can just relax with it, and that it is not about her. It is a victory for me to just stay with it myself and relax in Being and see it dissolving. That creates a sense of expansion and ability to contain it and move through it.

Another issue for me has been to judge myself when I don't understand what Isabelle is sharing. I would be so hard on myself about that. Now, I just relax with my impulse to try and understand it, and relax with my tendency to think a lot of critical things about her or myself. Even if I can't understand everything, I can still sense her, and just hear her, which is most useful. I think this is more fruitful and useful than using communication techniques. It is not wrong to use those methods, and they can be helpful, but there is a deeper understanding and a deeper solution. When you are relaxing in Being, a communication technique will be much more effective.

Michael and Catherine: Not Sharing the Mental Noise

Michael and Catherine, whose experience I also shared in Chapter 2, have noticed a significant change in their communication since they recognized their true nature and started resting as that for short moments. They noticed that they no longer share what's going on in the mind stream—all the conditioned ideas, expectations, disappointments, and reactions. Neither of them wants to communicate the mental noise in their head, knowing that is not what is most true. They would rather rest with that and, after it settles, see if something needs to be said.

Catherine explains, "We used to always try to work it out on the level of the mind, because that is all we knew. We were always processing things. It took so much energy and never really resolved anything. Now we are no longer processing all the time. We are mostly just allowing whatever arises to be *as it is* in the short moments, rather than bring it to each other. Sometimes there is clarity to say something. When I do say something, the way I communicate is entirely different. I may start off sharing, 'I may not see this clearly, but I would really like to discuss it. This is what I am sensing. What do you see?' I never did that before. That's a new way of communicating for me."

Michael notices that not only has Catherine's language changed, but also the energy that comes with her communication has changed, which he is sensitive to. He says, "In the past, when Catherine would want to discuss something, there would be an energy of annoyance. So, then right away, I would brace myself and think, *I'm in trouble.* Now, she will say, 'Michael, I want to talk about something.' The bells go off and the old habit of shrinking inside starts to happen, but when I relax in Being for a short moment, it just opens up again. Then, I can see that her sharing comes from a platform of real inquiry instead of, 'I don't like the way it is. I want it this way. What do we have to do to change it?' When she comes with openness, I am so much more able to meet her there."

Practicing Awakened Relating

Steve and Tracy: Building a Bubble of Safety in Relationship

Through their mutual commitment to remaining awake in the present moment while relating, Steve and his wife Tracy are building a container of safety in their relationship that allows them to be open, vulnerable, and honest with each other. When awakened relating is a priority, the defensive divided self is not in the foreground and we are more open and accepting with our self and our partner. When we know Undivided Love, we are free to tell the truth without fear and have the wisdom to know how to do that with clarity and compassion.

Steve and Tracy call this atmosphere of safety their "bubble." Being in a relationship with someone who shares their spiritual values and is making that the priority in life was an entirely new and exciting experience for them. The following conversation is with Steve, whom I supported in changing his old conditioned patterns of relating, which then paved the way for his relationship with Tracy.

When Steve was young, he became "the man of the house" for his single mother, who leaned on him in many ways. He learned to become an expert at taking care of her needs and ignoring his own. Steve's self-esteem became based on having others need and depend on him. He learned that relationship meant being what he called a "rescuer." Not surprisingly, Steve had a history of relationships with women who believed they needed to be rescued in some way.

His relationship with Tracy was the first one in his life that was not built on the old rescuer patterns. She supported him in the changes he was making in this pattern and in his commitment to be in an awakened partnership. Also, she did not need or want to be rescued.

Steve: Tracy and I have a mutual commitment to stay awake together and grow in that. Our primary commitment is to the ultimate truth. This is building what we call a "bubble" of safety in the relationship. We are continually learning more about how to live this truth, and revisiting how to better build the bubble. It's like building a house, one brick at a time.

LML: What are the "bricks" made of?

Steve: Other than the foundation of our commitment to ultimate truth and living as that, the main "brick" is the commitment to honest and open communication. As much as I thought I was a good listener in past relationships, I am a much better listener in my relationship with Tracy because of the safety we've created through our mutual commitment to staying awake in relationship and making that a priority. I can even hear Tracy talk about past relationships without being threatened. That was never the case before. Hearing about my partner's past relationships would feel like a threat; there would be some level of jealousy. Now, I feel very secure in who I am on the deepest level. I know who I truly am. I am more stable and solid in the wholeness of myself, so I am not threatened by anything she says. And, I know that all her past experiences are part of what led her to where she is now with me. That is true for me as well. I have come to see that all the experiences I went through in my past relationships, no matter how painful they were, made me willing to let go of my conditioned ways of relating and truly commit to a more awakened way of relating.

LML: Often, people fear that honest communication will threaten a relationship, but you found that it actually helps to build more safety, connection, and intimacy.

Steve: Tracy and I are discovering that the more open and totally honest we are with each other, the closer and more connected we feel, and the stronger the safety bubble becomes. This is true even when Tracy is upset with me and is sharing why she is upset. I am able to be present the whole time. I don't avoid anything or need to defend myself. I can just be present with her. I hear her and acknowledge why she is upset. It is okay for either of us to get angry and express that; we know that each of us is coming from a place of Love and allowing it all to be as it is. We trust that we are not wanting or trying to hurt each other, even if there is anger present. So, it feels safe. I know she is coming from love, even if she is angry.

LML: When it is coming from love, it is not only safe to hear the anger or upset, but it also creates a safety for it to be expressed in a way that allows it to be heard and released. This is healing for both of you.

Steve: Our spiritual commitment to awakened relating is what makes this possible. It is where we find the true safety. I couldn't have done it without that. I could not have built the bubble with Tracy without first having committed to a spiritual existence.

LML: We don't find the deepest safety in another person alone. We find it in the common ground of Being that we all share.

Steve: That is so much clearer to me now than it ever has been before. And, being in a relationship where there is a mutual commitment to this is making it even clearer. It is now obvious to me that the foundation for a healthy, intimate relationship is found in staying in conscious contact with the oneness, the wholeness, and our shared connectedness with the entire universe. This is the foundation. Knowing this has allowed me to relate to and see Tracy in her true essence. Having that connectedness, openness, and honesty and being completely present for each other is really sweet. It is a true connection—a heart to heart connection. It is an energetic embrace.

LML: Sharing our one Being consciously in close relationship is the fulfillment of human relating.

Steve: Yes, and it includes all relationships with all people and all of life. Life is about relationship. All I can say is that it feels right. It feels like I am finally coming home. I used to read the chapter on enlightened relationships in *The Power of Now* by Eckhart Tolle (1999) over and over again, longing to experience that, but it was abstract for me. Now, I have some experience with enlightened or awakened relating directly. It has come alive for me. Instead of relating from the ego "me" and the pain body, we can relate from the deeper presence. I am so grateful for this adventure!

MEDITATIVE INQUIRY:
Practice Telling the Truth

Commit for just one day at a time to practice telling the truth to yourself and then to your partner or a friend. By truth I mean that which is most authentic from your heart, rather than from the conditioned mind. Notice all the ways in which you are not telling the full truth. Pay attention to why. Are you afraid of offending them? Are you afraid of rejection? Are you afraid of being shamed? Just notice.

When you don't tell the truth, take a moment to touch into what *is* true. Drop down into your body. Let go of the thinking mind and all its stories about what is going on. Just feel into the sensations in the body and be as fully present as possible in the moment. You might find discomfort in the form of intensity or tightness in your chest or belly. You might find feelings of insecurity, unworthiness, or fear. You may also drop into a direct experience of the deepest truth, the pure space of Being, which is more fundamentally true than any of our temporary feelings or sensations. Just be with the truest experience you know in the moment. Begin with telling yourself this truth.

Once you tell yourself the truth, I invite you to practice telling the truth with others, even when it feels scary or vulnerable, and see what happens. Notice how it is to communicate from an undefended heart. Does it create more closeness or does it create conflict? If conflict is created, look at where your communication was coming from within you. Were you coming from Love or fear? Were you speaking as an undivided heart or as the conditioned mind? If you've created more closeness, take that in. Feel it in your body and notice how it feels to relate this way so your body-mind can learn to trust that it is safe to tell the truth.

CHAPTER 9

One Love, Two Bodies
Awakened Sexuality

*Sex has a higher potential—sex is able to carry us beyond
duality into a spiritual unity that brings us closer to
ourselves, the other, nature, and God.*

—Diana Richardson

There is only one primordial life force expressing itself in a multitude
of ways. The most powerful expression of this life force in the human
body is sexual energy. It has the potency to bring about the creation of
life and to lift the expression of human love into an exalted and sacred
experience. Sexual energy also has the power to be harmful when it is
not channeled through our heart essence. Misuse of sexual energy has
caused immense suffering in our world. However, if we learn to experience its highest potential, our sexual energy can increase our joy, love,
and connection, as well as deepen our awakening to our true nature.

Religious doctrine and cultural norms have attempted to repress
sexual energy throughout history. This repression has often led to
destructive expressions of this potent energy, which naturally wants to
move freely. Due to the Internet, pornography now has a strong influ-
ence on sexuality in our world. Unfortunately, this is taking humanity
farther away from learning how to allow sexual energy to move freely
in a harmonious, healthy way. Elwood Watson (2014) writes:

> What is notable is the fact that 90 percent of young boys and
> 60 percent of young girls have been exposed to pornography
> before they reach the age of eighteen. … The median age that

children become introduced to such material is eleven years old! … In certain segments of society, sexual abuse and some cases, rape is steadily increasing. While pornography addiction cannot be blamed as the sole reason for these issues, it is likely to be a contributing factor.

Sexuality is not something to be avoided, nor is it something to indulge in unconsciously. When sexual energy is allowed to be as it is, it naturally flows as Love. But, there are so many potential obstacles that can block this flow. Most of us have been conditioned by belief systems that instill guilt, fear, insecurity, and shame around sexuality. This conditioning can keep the vast potential of sexuality imprisoned in a cage of painful, limited expression.

Sexual energy holds the same sacred intent of all of life and nature, which is to return to our primordial unity. In addition to the biological pull for procreation and pleasure, there is an even deeper need to experience the oneness of our shared Being. Sexual union is the closest we can come to that unity short of knowing and sharing Undivided Love. Yet, sexual union alone inevitably falls short of fulfilling our longing for union with our true nature.

In a conversation I had with Rupert Spira (2014), he discussed this longing for union with our innermost Self and awakened sexuality.

Even the porn industry, one of the largest industries in the world, is fueled ultimately by the longing for our true nature, that is, by the desire to be divested of all limitations and to be returned to our original innocence, nakedness, and freedom. The desire for sexual intimacy is really the longing for peace, happiness, and love. Sexual intimacy may indeed bring about a temporary loss of the feeling of separation, albeit a partial loss, but it does not uproot the origin of the feeling, and therefore the desire returns again and again. In fact, the French phrase for orgasm is "le petite mort," meaning "little death." The moment of orgasm is a merging or losing of oneself; it is a "little death" of everything that limits us. That is the impulse behind most people's desire for sexual intimacy. Most people don't realize it, but what they are really seeking in sexual intimacy is to lose themselves in that timeless moment. Of course, sexual intimacy can also be a means of sharing and expressing the true intimacy of Love. That is awakened sexuality.

As we learn to more fully allow and be present with our sexuality—without either repressing or indulging—we can begin to touch the sacredness of it. Sex can be experienced as an exquisite blending of human love and infinite Love in a natural flow of grace and beauty. This is the marriage of emptiness and form, or Shiva and Shakti, which is the essence of many tantra teachings. First, we experience this marriage within our self and then we can share it in union with our beloved. Spiritual teacher David Spero (2015) beautifully expresses this as "our own Being making love to itself, which is the highest form of tantra. It's what all tantra points to: the inner alchemical transformation whereby the energy within your own Being makes love to itself." To share this exquisite inner lovemaking in a bodily embrace with another human being is an ultimate expression of awakened sexuality.

Qualities of Awakened Sexuality

Awakened sexuality has a very different quality from our conventional experiences of sexuality. Awakened sexuality has the potential to bring us to far greater expressions of Love and unity than can be experienced in duality. Sex that is grounded in awakened Love takes us beyond the realm of our conditioned, separate identities into a true intimacy in the wholeness of shared Being. At the same time, awakened sex includes all our humanness, with its conditioning, emotions, wounding, and learned sexual habits. Awakened sexuality is a coupling of our human and divine natures.

Awakened sexuality is about being present in the moment and in the body without an agenda. Conventional sex is usually about performance and reaching a goal—orgasm. The focus is on "doing" rather than simply "being." All the doing involved in conventional sex takes us away from the direct experience of our shared Being, where true intimacy is found. Therefore, it will ultimately lead to dissatisfaction and disconnectedness. When we do not allow our lovemaking to evolve and expand within the boundless expanse of Undivided Love, it can become routine, mechanical, and predictable. The boredom ultimately leads to a search for different partners or a desire to go to more and more extremes to find excitement, which is never truly satisfying.

There are so many expectations around sexuality. We tend to believe that something is wrong if sex is not happening frequently or is not always passionate and exciting. As we tap into the infinite pleasure of true Love, making love is alive from moment to moment, which never becomes routine and is always beautiful whether it is intense and passionate or a soft, quiet meditation. It has its own flow that is unique to each couple, which may be frequent, infrequent, or varying. The frequency of sex doesn't matter. What matters is allowing and appreciating its natural movement.

The following chart highlights the differences between what is typically experienced in conventional sex and the potential of sexuality as it continues to evolve into a more awakened expression of this energy. Of course, awakened sexuality can contain elements of conventional sex and vice versa. For most people, it is a mixture of the two as we evolve towards a more natural expression of our sexual nature, inspired by presence and unobstructed by beliefs and convention.

Conventional Sexuality	Awakened Sexuality
Doing	Being
Based in gratification of needs	Based in Love
Agendas and goals, future focus	No goal, no agenda, in present moment
Tension and constriction	Relaxation and flow
Fast, hard movement	Slow, soft movement
Avoidance of painful experience	Fully allowing all experience

Attachment to other as source of Love	Connection with true source of Love
Ego involvement in performance	Humility and surrender to what is
Insecurity and fear	Confidence and trust in deeper nature
Contrived, forced, unspontaneous	Uncontrived, free, spontaneous
Emotionally defended	Undefended and open
Focused in mind	Being present in body and heart
Moving from conditioned mind	Moving from stillness and presence

The qualities of awakened sexuality will arise naturally as we let go into our heart essence when we come together to make love. There is no need to struggle and strive towards this. It will unfold naturally the more we awaken to our essence and relax together. In fact, the more that effort is involved, the more it interferes with the open, allowing quality of awakened sexuality and intimacy. As our experience evolves, it will effortlessly take on more of the qualities of awakened sexuality, and the painful aspects of conventional sex will fall away on their own. It is important to be gentle with yourself and start where you are, taking whatever you see as your next step toward a more awakened sexuality.

In preparation for this chapter, I asked many couples if they would be willing to talk about their experience with awakened sexuality. I was not looking for "sexperts," just people who were sincerely trying to bring some level of awakened consciousness to their sexual relationships. Since this is such a new exploration for all of us, it was difficult to find couples that felt confident enough to discuss their experience with awakened sexuality. So John and I decided to share our experience, even though this is new for us as well. It feels vulnerable to share this intimate process, yet we do so in hopes of benefitting others by sharing the evolution of our sexual relating into a more awakened sexuality.

John and Lynn Marie: Sex as a Doorway to Healing and Awakening

Exploring awakened sexuality has been a doorway into deeper Love and healing for both John and me. This area of our relationship has needed attention, healing, kindness, and patience. We are both grateful to have found a willing partner in each other for this exploration. It has been a spiritual practice for us, which has been as transformative as it has been challenging. Through dedication, love, and perseverance, our sexual relating is opening up to be a purer expression of Love and beauty.

It is rare to have any healthy conditioning around sexuality; it has been so distorted throughout most of human history. Neither of us had any sex education in school or at home. It just wasn't available. We had to figure it out ourselves. Even today, sex education is not adequate, and too many young people are being educated by pornography, which is a highly distorted version of sexuality and intimacy.

My early experiences of sex did not include being fully present and in touch with my body, feelings, or my partners. It wasn't until I met John that I felt safe enough to begin to be more present with sexual experience. From the beginning, being with John was like coming home to a deep safety that I had always longed for. However, as I came more into my body and into the moment while making love, it was initially a challenge to be truly present to all the difficult sensations and feelings that can arise in this potent, intimate sharing. Yet, I didn't want to escape it anymore. We are both committed to our spiritual awakening, so it felt natural to include sexuality in that process. It no longer felt right for me to practice being present in my life without making sex a part of that.

It is amazing how much can arise with sexual contact—both ecstatic pleasure and deep emotional pain. We all hold a lot of pain around sexuality, especially women. Being present in the moment sexually is not just about pleasure; it can also be about healing and awakening. Sex is a healing modality; it is medicine. We can heal in an embrace of Love, presence, and compassion. When we consciously use the power of sexual energy, it purges all the old pain in a deep safety and opens the heart to the one Love we all are. In a conversation I had with Carla, a tantric teacher whose story I shared in Chapter 1, she related:

> We all have so much pain around intimacy and sexuality. We try not to feel the pain that may arise in the present moment. The pain can make it difficult to relax into the deeper Presence. Like a magnifying glass, sexuality can bring up all the issues you have in your life and in relationship. It makes them all more vivid and clear. Yet, facing the feelings or issues is always an opening to a deeper level of contact. It is an opportunity to be more sensitive, more vulnerable, more open, and more human.

It is important to remember that, when we open to all that arises, whether painful or pleasurable, it becomes a doorway to deeper intimacy and awakening. Initially, being more in the present moment with sexual experience brought up emotions that were difficult to be with, such as shame, disgust, fear, and anger. It also brought up blissful joy, ecstatic pleasure, and of course, Love. It was essential to focus on awakened awareness, while allowing the difficult feelings to pass through. This is what made it possible. Over time, the difficult feelings moved through and we were able to open more fully into the unity of true Love together and enjoy more love, bliss, and pleasure. No matter what came up, when it was met with presence and loving acceptance, it became a doorway to more Love and healing. As John says, "This is a sensitive, loving practice that we joyfully take our time with as we learn to bring our wakefulness into our sexual relationship. It is an ongoing process of being with both the beauty and the pain of coming into the sheer intimacy of the moment together."

We found that what worked for us was making a commitment to just be together on a regular basis, without any agenda. We would just come together and be open to whatever happened. We gave each other permission to not be sexual if it did not feel right. We only needed to commit to being open, honest, and allowing. Even if no sexual contact occurred, being together in this way was intimate, vulnerable, and real. It always feels like making love—and it is. These shared, healing moments are bringing Love to all the parts of us that hold pain and hurt around sexuality. And, it is deepening our connection and our capacity for intimacy. In John's words, "It is all just beautiful. The closeness, the intimacy, the way the energies can build and fall back and then build again, or not. The depth of satisfaction and closeness is incomparable to anything I ever experienced formerly with conventional sex."

There are "tools" that help us be more present in our bodies and in the moment. Remembering to breathe in the belly and staying in communication is important, and so is frequent eye contact. Maintaining eye contact keeps us connected not only with each other, but also with the one Being we share. At first, it felt too vulnerable to remain in eye contact. Now, I am able to relax into the gaze of shared Being. It is also helpful to stay present by communicating our experience in words or sounds, especially what feels good. Emphasizing what feels positive helps us to be with more difficult feelings and sensations.

The most important thing we've discovered is to remain in our shared heart essence. We keep coming back to that as often as needed. That is the most important thing. All the other tools are just to support that. We practice remaining as our essence in daily life so that all our interactions, including lovemaking, can come from that place. As John says, "When I am resting in the clear, open space of my own Being—when we meet *here*—whatever is happening, whether it is ecstatic sex or a seemingly mundane conversation, we are making Love. The result is always more Love in this world that we share with everyone."

Practicing Awakened Relating

Marlies: The Dance of Shiva and Shakti

For many years, Marlies has been dedicated to the healing and awakening of sexuality for herself and others. She is a spiritual teacher, therapist, and teacher of sacred sexuality. Sacred sexuality involves the union and liberation of the two aspects of consciousness and matter— Shiva and Shakti. As Marlies says, "Shiva is the masculine quality— the emptiness or pure awareness. And Shakti is form—any feeling, sensation, movement, or expression that comes out of Shiva. They come together as one and complement each other."

Marlies and I have taught workshops together on awakened relationships. I have also attended her powerful sexual healing retreats for women. She has helped John and me understand awakened sexuality more deeply. I appreciate her openness on this subject and the depth of her understanding and experience. Marlies and I had the following conversation about awakened sexuality. I began by asking what "awakened sexuality" means to her.

Marlies: First of all, in order to experience awakened sexuality, you must have some degree of awakening to your true nature so that you know that you are not your body, mind, and personality, and simultaneously, you are all that, too. In my experience, it is living in what I call a "space body" that is full of emptiness and full of life. We need to come to really, really know who we truly are. That is the ground of awakened sexuality, awakened relating, and awakened life. Then, once that is known, it is bringing that into the sexual realm. This requires an embodied awakening, not just transcendence of the body-mind. When we realize our awakening in the body and become an expression of that Love, then we can bring that into sexual contact. Before we can bring awakening to sex with another, we need to have some intimacy with all of life, which is really quite sexual. In that intimacy with life you taste everything so completely. It is the same taste— being with a tree, or anything else—as it is being with another human. There can be an intimacy with all of life.

When we come together in lovemaking with this true intimacy, we have no goals. That is not how we are trained. We are trained to believe that when we come together with someone sexually, there are so many expectations. For a female it might be, "I need to be hot, I need to be excited, and I need to be wet." For a man, it might be, "I need to have a hard on, I need to perform," and many other expectations. My experience is that you only need to show up. You only need to show up and agree to spend this time together. Then, you step into a sacred space. I step into a room where Shiva and Shakti come together, from within and without. For me, that is the flavor of awakened sexuality. The invitation is to show up and rest as Being as much as you can, or just rest in your belly, and let the bodies make love, not the mind. Dare to dive into the unknown!

Because there is no goal, awakened sexuality is being with whatever is here—super enjoyable, super painful, whatever it is. As we relax as that wakefulness, all is received in this wakeful body, in this wakeful Being. When you come together in awakened sexuality, my experience is that there is not another body. There clearly appears to be another body there, but I can see that I am this body *and* I am the apparent other body. There is oneness. From the outside, it could look like conventional sex because two bodies are moving together, but it's experienced as one Love moving as two bodies. We are moving as the vibration of the one Being that we are. The more I stay with my direct experience, the more openness there is to the intimacy I experience with the partner who seems to be outside myself. For me, it is mostly males. But, it really doesn't matter if it is a male or female partner; it is really just two humans coming together.

LML: What led you to put so much focus on working with sexuality?

Marlies: Basically, I got interested in working with sexuality because I was raped a few times when I was younger. There was so much pain and I always felt that something was missing when I made love. So, I started healing my sexuality and that brought me into contact with Barry Long, a tantric master, who really helped me a lot. Also, I had a practice partner at the time. We were not in love, but we loved each other, and we practiced together. I really learned to stay still inside. That is the most important thing. We all get constant input from the media that with sex, we need to go faster and harder. For me, awakened lovemaking is really about slowing down. It is about becoming so still inside that I am really in the body, in the senses, and not in the psychological thoughts and feelings on top of that. When we are truly in the body in this way, then the bodies can start making love. It is not the mind making love. For many people, the mind makes love and it is what I call "friction sex." When the bodies make love, there is union with each other and you become this one movement together.

When I started practicing this new way of making love, what I noticed in the beginning was that even though there was a willingness to move as wakefulness, I was trained to focus on what didn't feel good. It was very hard for me to move from naturalness and goodness, because there was so much pain and discomfort. Barry Long helped me to focus on the goodness. He said, "Just rest as your Self and start naming the goodness." He would give me examples of goodness, like, "It is so nice to look into your eyes," or, "I appreciate your touch." He suggested that, for a while, I just don't focus on the negative, like my fears and pain, but to just focus on the goodness that is happening in each moment. That has been very important to me. I'm not talking about being in denial. The more I rest in the Being that I am, the more naturally it expresses itself as the goodness of allowing all that is, which leads to falling into the oneness of Being together.

LML: Can you speak about the difference between conventional sexuality and awakened sexuality?

Marlies: Yes, there is a big difference. Conventional sexuality has a goal and as I already mentioned, awakened sexuality has no goal. It is always different and it is about relaxation. Orgasms may come, but they don't come from friction, they come from relaxation. Those orgasms nourish you, so you come away from lovemaking nourished, instead of depleted. Most people are not even aware of how different sexuality can truly be. Most people make love for a very short period of time, maybe just a few minutes. It is mostly just a release. You are depleted, so you fall asleep. Something has relaxed. That's nice, but it is not nourishing. For me, awakened sexuality is very nourishing. Orgasms happen, but you step together into the realm of Shiva and Shakti, the realm of wakefulness, and see what wants to happen. Maybe what wants to happen is to just hold each other. Or maybe intercourse happens. It doesn't matter. The focus is on staying in the wakefulness of the moment and seeing what wants to happen spontaneously.

LML: Are there any tools or guidance you can give people to help them awaken to the energy of wakefulness or stillness, and to stay as that when they make love?

Marlies: It is important that we connect with the stillness of our true nature in awakened lovemaking. The stillness is always present. To connect with it, go inside and close your eyes and just sense your body—not your thoughts about your body, but your direct experience of your body. Be with whatever is, pleasure or pain, without the judgment on top of it. Be with the energy of the body. Also, most people can find energy in their hands and feel that as an entryway to the energy of the body. When we sit quietly and bring our focus within our body, most people can find the stillness of their Being, even though we are not trained to find it. Once that stillness is found, it is about resting as that. That is what takes practice, as well as presence and Love. It is just resting here as that presence and Love and not moving from that.

LML: The stillness is not far away. We tend to think that it is something so special and unavailable. It is actually right here, in a moment of deep relaxation.

Marlies: Absolutely. This is also true for lovemaking. We are trained to think that lovemaking has to become some really big, special thing. When really, it is very simple. Within that simplicity there can be ecstasy and there can be stillness. It can be a very quiet, deep vibration, so you need to be very quiet and still to allow the sacred vibrations of the yoni to come to life. The hard pounding of conventional sex is what kills that. Even for myself, I was trained to have sex that way. I always knew that there was something wrong with that, but I didn't know what else to do until someone told me about a different way. I am so grateful that I happened to have some good teachers, including some wonderful male teachers. That has been a tremendous gift.

For years, I have been pondering why I have met only a handful of men who are willing to explore awakened sexuality. I know many men who are so afraid. I know many very awake, beautiful men who are afraid to just be still and present in sexuality.

LML: Why do you think many men are afraid of this?

Marlies: I think that men are afraid of not performing well. It is so scary for them. It is so deeply engrained that they need to perform. Especially when men are into friction sex, they want the penis to be very hard and they are afraid of losing that. But, the more you come into awakened sexuality, the penis becomes what I call "soft-hard." And, the yoni becomes softer also. Everything relaxes and is softer.

This can be scary for men because there tends to be a period of time when they just lose their erection. Something dies. It is fantastic when it dies, but this is frightening for the man. When the old goals of sex have died, then a man can really step into lovemaking that is new, that has no direction, no goal, and comes from relaxation. The erections will come back, but in a new way. The tissues will be softer; they are less hard. This is where it can be important for the female to let the man know that this is truly okay.

LML: I get the feel of what you are saying. It involves relaxing, slowing down, and being sensitive and present right here and now.

Marlies: Yes, and this really takes a deep willingness. I see this as a practice for the rest of my life, just like staying awake in life is a daily practice. For me, it is about making love to all of life. With sexual love, you offer yourself up to space and to each other, and then are curious about how that wants to move and express itself. It is an utter willingness to rest in one's Self, no matter what happens, or does not happen.

Then within that willingness an intimacy arises. For me, that intimacy is with whatever is in the moment. There is always a quality of waiting. We come together, and then like the out breath, we just wait until the dance of the bodies wants to happen. The bodies want to dance and we are not in charge of that.

I think as a species, we are maturing and becoming more ready to evolve our sexuality. But there is still so much perversion of sexuality in our world. I think the porn industry, sex trafficking, abuse, and rape have increased since the Internet was created. Simultaneously, more and more people are getting interested in healthier lovemaking and sexuality. We are becoming ready to let go of the old ways of making love and let that die. It is a death of what you know yourself to be in your sexuality. It is also daring to step into the mystery. This death is an evolutionary leap. It is a death of an era, of a certain quality of consciousness.

The beauty of awakened sexuality is that the female becomes one yoni, or one vagina, a receiver like a flower, and the male becomes one penis, or wand of light as a giver. Of course, giving and receiving can blend together and then we do not know who is the giver and who is the receiver. As we evolve into awakened sexuality, the wand of the man will come into the vagina of the woman, filling it with healing light and taking out the pain. With this process, a woman can get quite emotional. But, if a man stays present as pure awareness, then the pain and emotions are absorbed by pure awareness. Then, more and more you can make love from the natural felt-sense of the body, free of the pain of the psychological and emotional bodies.

This is also true for same-sex partners who have a commitment to being awake in their lovemaking. Whether the couple is heterosexual or homosexual, there is a natural polarity of masculine and feminine, because that is what attracts them to each other.

LML: This can be deeply healing for the female pain body that holds so much wounding in our world. There is so much wounding around sexuality for both men and women.

Marlies: It is both healing and nourishing, and, yet, when we come together in awakened lovemaking, it is not about working on anything. It is not about processing our pain. It is just pure awareness receiving everything that comes. It receives it and allows it to flow in and out, and then it releases. Then you don't stay stuck in anything anymore. It just comes and it goes. It is being touched, deeply touched. It is daring to really be touched and not know what the heck is going to happen. For myself, I need to learn that too. I can sometimes think I need to have it together and be in control. So, it is a dying of that idea, too. You will start moving and you don't know why you are moving in that way. It is free. You don't need your mind anymore, you just move. It is really a dance.

LML: It is a spontaneous dance coming freely out of the moment, which is how life is meant to be.

Marlies: Absolutely, I agree. Sacred sexuality is about saying "yes" to everything. In a way, that is what lovemaking is—an utter "yes" to all of life. It is an utter receiving and tasting, an intimacy with everything.

MEDITATIVE INQUIRY:
Awakened Lovemaking Meditation

The following meditation is adapted with permission from the "Erotic Meditation" developed by tantra educator Lyn Hunstead.

Sit with a partner and take all the time you need to drop into the stillness in the body. If you have access to the stillness of Being, rest as that. If you do not have access in this moment, then take time to just notice that the body is still inside, or ask, "What is already still?" Feel into that and relax. Or, you can simply breathe deeply in your belly.

Once you are grounded in stillness, or in the present moment, take turns being the giver and receiver for a set amount of time. The receiver rests as awareness and remains present to the touch with eyes closed. The giver may also want to keep the eyes closed, at least some of the time, in order to stay in touch with the stillness inside. This can be done while both are sitting up, or with the receiver lying down.

Receiver, be sure that you make any boundaries you want to keep known to the giver. Giver, before you touch your partner, take a moment to notice your breath and drop deeper into the stillness. When you feel ready, allow your hands to touch your partner's body in whatever way feels like a natural flow, a spontaneous movement of Love. Enter into the felt sense of the movements, becoming one with them and allowing them to move as waves in the ocean, ever-changing, never knowing how the next wave will unfold. If you find yourself moving or touching in a way that seems too habitual, stop, reconnect with the openness of the underlying stillness, and allow your movement to come from there. Then, start moving outside of the realm of mind, which makes every movement fresh and new.

This movement has no goal and no direction. Again and again, both the giver and receiver can let go of all agendas and expectations. It doesn't matter how much movement occurs. Just stay present in the body. What is most important is to practice resting as stillness while moving. When we start moving as stillness, or awareness, the movement tends to be very slow and opens the sensual body naturally as we come into our senses.

While staying present in the stillness, the giver is advised to be open and curious about what brings the receiver more pleasure. Continue to dance with these pleasurable sensations, then move back into deep stillness together. After each person gets a turn being a giver and receiver, end this practice with a "Namaste" bow to your other Self.

PART III

Living Undivided
Love Together

CHAPTER 10

Living Love
Staying Awake Together

The commitment is much more than to one another. It is really a commitment to living truth. That's a more fundamental commitment.

—John Prendergast

Whether we are conscious of it or not, we are all the embodiment of living Love. When we are relating to life and each other from Love, it naturally shines forth. We find Love through being it. We find more Love by living life from or *as* the truth of our Being. The way to experience awakened relating is to *be* the Undivided Love of our shared Being and live as that. It doesn't matter if we are not yet consciously living this at all times; it begins with moments of living Love that grow into the continuous flow that is its natural expression.

When we relate *as* Love, we experience and express qualities such as unconditional acceptance, compassion, openness, integrity, honesty, humility, trust, respect, clarity, wisdom, and spaciousness. When we relate as an imaginary divided self that is trying to get love and have our needs met from another, we tend to be fearful, judgmental, dependent, insecure, controlling, jealous, manipulative, defensive, and reactive. When we discover the source of Love and let go of the demand that relationship must produce love and ultimate fulfillment, then Love can flow naturally. In awakened relating, we allow Love to inform how we relate. We relax as the open expanse of Love, and allow it to inspire our body, speech, mind, and behavior.

We are not able to stay awake together when we relate through the filters of our conditioned patterns, rather than from unconditioned Love. The conditioned mind only knows its programming, which is not alive and awake in the moment. It involves living from old, worn out habitual points of view. We relate according to how we have been taught to relate until we wake up out of that. And, as I have said, waking up to our true nature will not magically dissolve all our conditioning. We must allow our conditioning to rest in the ground of awakeness as it arises in relationship again and again for it to resolve or transform. This is the dynamic living process of awakened relating.

We are also not able to stay awake together when we relate from a divided self that is more interested in getting its needs met than experiencing real Love. The divided self only knows about avoiding pain and seeking pleasure. It tries to manage the pain of separation through utilizing defensive strategies and manipulating our partner to be the way we imagine they should be, rather than relaxing into openhearted relating. We are not awake in our relating if we are resisting or controlling our experience or our partner in any way. Yet, if we are knowingly awake to Undivided Love, none of these painful forms of relating are necessary. They may still arise out of habit, but they can be seen for what they are and released in the light of awareness.

Getting Our Priorities Straight

I have found in my own experience that an essential element of awakened relating is to make awakening to our true nature the number one priority. This means prioritizing and fully committing to whatever level of recognition we have in this moment—whether it is one glimpse or a continuous flow of awakened awareness. It can begin with one short moment of resting in spacious awareness or relaxing into the deepest truth you know in the moment, with the intention of full commitment behind it. It is the *intention* that is important. Our ability to stay awake in our relating will certainly grow in this committed intention.

Once we recognize the source of Love, it is important to commit to resting as that and relying on it as much as possible for love, wisdom, comfort, and solutions to all issues that life brings to us. We make it a priority to remind ourselves, and our partner, to rely on the infinite wisdom of the source rather than on our limited, divided identities. This commitment becomes easier as we begin to realize that there is nothing outside of or other than our basic nature. We can see through our own observing awareness that prioritizing anything else while ignoring the source fails to provide a lasting solution every time. And, we can also see through our own observation that when we rest as and rely on the source, it never fails us. The deepest truth is that there is really nothing else to turn to! Over time, we naturally become devoted to this sacred presence that is always holding us in a palpable field of Undivided Love.

We can look at our own life to show us what our priorities are and whether it is time to reconsider them. We simply notice where we place our attention most of the time. How much is our attention being brought to rest in Being, and how much is it going out towards people, activities, thoughts, states of mind, and objects? We give our attention to what is most important to us. If our attention is focused outward on getting love from our partner while ignoring the true source of Love, our partner is the priority. The same is true of our work, or any other activity. Take an honest look and ask, "What am I devoted to?" If attention is absorbed in thoughts most of the time, then thoughts are what we are devoted to. It takes courage, honesty, and integrity to tell ourselves the truth and closely examine what we have been making the priority in our lives. It is not about never focusing on thoughts, feelings, our partner, work, or anything else, it is about *prioritizing* and *emphasizing* the ground of Being, while allowing all that arises to be fully experienced.

As awakening becomes our number one priority, we are willing to let go of our ego's defenses in the moments when we are challenged, which, as we all know, can be frequent in an intimate relationship. This willingness allows us to open and relax when the ego-self is screaming at us to defend, attack, or shut down. We need a strong willingness to not go with these impulses when they are activated. In those moments, we can ask, "Is it more important to be awake, or is it more important to defend my imagined separate self right now?" If awakening is not the priority, we may succumb to the pull of the ego to be right and defend rather than rest and respond from clarity. For most of us, it takes practice to remain stable during our emotional reactions.

This practice involves relying on something other than our conditioned mind. Since our habit of relying on the conditioned mind is so strong, it usually requires returning to the unconditioned, infinite intelligence repeatedly until those habits begin to subside or dissolve. This is not a casual process. It takes a deep commitment to stay awake. I have heard people say, "But that is so much work!" It can seem so at first. Our conditioned identity has a tremendous momentum. It requires commitment and effort to bring our attention out of the conditioned mind in the beginning. However, the more we stay with it, the easier it gets. What will never get easier is maintaining the sense of a separate self. That takes energy and constant effort. Relaxing into our true nature releases that energy and we no longer feel compelled to make the constant efforts needed to maintain this imagined self. It is important to realize that living as a conditioned identity is a lot more difficult than making the commitment to staying awake.

All the couples and individuals whose stories of awakened relating I share in this book have a commitment to prioritizing awakening in relationship. If each partner shares this commitment, it is a gift and a blessing. However, it is not necessary for both people in a relationship to be equally committed or to have equal levels of spiritual understanding to experience awakened relating. The only thing that is essential is your own willingness to make awakening a priority in your life, whether your partner chooses to or not. We cannot blame an unconscious partner for our own unconsciousness. No matter where they are at, we are responsible only for our own experience. If we do not have support for awakened relating from our partner, we can find support outside the relationship. Or, our commitment may lead us to another relationship that supports this more fully. When we make the commitment in our heart, life provides us with all we need for our awakening.

Helping Each Other Stay Awake

Because of our shared commitment, John and I help each other stay awake in the relationship as much as possible. When one of us gets lost and goes into a reaction of some kind, the other often calls attention to what we really care about and what is actually true. One thing that John has often asked me when I am in an emotional reaction is, "What is most important to you?" This usually brings me right back, even while I'm experiencing charged feelings. The charged feeling may remain, but I am reminded of the truth underlying it, which makes it possible to allow my feelings to be there without getting lost in them. Instead of engaging in each other's reactions in some way, we simply remind each other of our commitment. We can then address what is going on from a place of clarity. Of course, in some moments this is a lot easier said than done! But, we strengthen our "clarity muscle" by using it.

Throughout our relationship, John and I have found ways to remind each other to stay present and awake to what is most true. One of the first tools I remember we used at the beginning of our relationship is touching a finger to our nose when the other was caught up in a story and their point of view. This meant, "Don't touch the story." Not touching the story means not engaging the story as though it is the full reality and truth of "what is" in the moment. None of the stories in our mind are the whole truth. They are not the whole truth because they represent our limited perspective that is shaped by our conditioning, our projection, and our interpretation of the situation. The whole truth always emerges from the ground of Being, which we lose touch with when we believe our stories and hold on to them tightly. Our ego doesn't like seeing this reminder when we are caught up in a story. However, if the deeper commitment is there, we have the willingness to drop it or move toward seeing it from a larger vantage point.

Another tool we have used when one of us is forgetting what is true and is caught up in a reaction or believing a story, is to speak or shout the Tibetan Buddhist syllable PHAT (we pronounce it "PET").

PHAT is a sacred syllable that has been used to shock the mind back into the immediacy of vivid wakefulness when it has gotten engaged in making thoughts, feelings, or fantasies real and separate from the ground they are arising in. When one of us is engaged in a story about the other that is fully believed, we have lost direct contact with the ground of Being. This takes us out of the spacious perspective that undivided awareness provides and into a narrow, limited perspective that is not wholly true. The PHAT syllable or nose touching reminders are usually sufficient for either John or me to stop and drop into the deeper truth that is always here, providing clarity and wisdom for whatever needs attention. The story and reactions may still be going on, but they can be addressed from a spacious clarity, rather than from a constricted reactivity.

Our friends Margo and John, whose story is in Chapter 12, have also developed playful tools to help each other stay awake to what is most true in relationship. One of their favorites is what they refer to as "tic-toc." This is a reminder to slow down and come into the present moment. When one of them is caught up in a big to-do list and becomes grumpy about all they have to do, or about the other not doing things fast enough, they say, "tic-toc." This reminds them to take a moment to rest in present moment awareness. They also have a clock that chimes in the center of their house every fifteen minutes as a reminder to call them home to their true nature. Another tool they use when one of them gets triggered and reactive is for the other to call out "reset." Then, they both stop and take a brief moment to rest in the loving expanse of the field of awareness. At that point, the reactivity is either released or they are able to clearly communicate about it. They report that this saves a lot of time that would otherwise be spent processing together.

Similar to the tool "reset" is "love alert," which they use as a way to call each other back to the one field of Love that they share. When one of them says "love alert" they stop and gaze into each other's eyes for a brief time until they are once again conscious of shared Being. This quickly brings Margo and John back to the true Love of their nature that they share, especially since they have been practicing eye gazing with each other for many years. Eye gazing is a powerful practice that supports awakened relating. It both helps us recognize our shared Being and assists us in relating as that. I describe the practice of eye gazing in the Meditative Inquiry at the end of Chapter 11.

When we fall into old, negative, and conditioned patterns in relationship, we can always remind each other to raise our vibration by focusing on our highest intention to *be* Love or what we Love and appreciate about our partner. This is choosing to transcend negativity by doing whatever we can to focus on what is positive and inspiring. If we have one hundred percent commitment to *being* Love, there is always something we can come up with that we appreciate about our partner. Focusing on that opens up the flow of Love again.

It doesn't matter what words or behaviors are used as reminders, you can use any of these examples or make up your own. What is important is that they shake us out of the trance of believing our thought stories and bring us into the clear, open space of now. In addition to using tools to help each other stay awake, it is important to support our commitment in any way we can. John and I support this priority in many ways, including a daily sitting practice, remembering to rest as present awareness throughout the day, reading and listening to teachings, being with teachers, taking time out to be on retreat, spending time in nature, and being in community with others who have this commitment. This is another important aspect of commitment. Without support and reminders, we may get lost in the strong habitual tendencies that arise in relationship and in life. This can be true even for people who have a stable sense of awakened awareness.

The following interview with John and Christiane is an example of a couple with a deep, shared commitment and understanding that allows them to be with the ever-changing flow of experience in relationship while maintaining contact with the constancy of Being. Their deeper knowing makes it possible for them to fully allow whatever stories may arise between them to be as they are, even with emotional intensity, while simultaneously knowing that it is not the absolute truth. This has the power to unravel their conditioned identities while strengthening their commitment to stand together in Truth.

In order to not get lost in the story, we shift our attention from the story to the observing awareness of the story, while emphasizing and prioritizing that. This may need to be practiced repeatedly over time before we can fully allow the story without getting caught in it. We mature into more freedom as we stop identifying with the thoughts that create the stories and begin to identify as the impersonal, awake awareness that is always free.

Within the wholeness of Being, it is possible to allow our stories and their emotional reactions to flower and unfold their true, underlying beneficial nature. Eventually, we come to know that everything arises from the deepest truth of life, abides within that for a while, and then dissolves back into it, becoming a beneficial offering for whatever is needed in the moment. Anything we fully allow will return us to clarity, not only on the absolute level, but also on the relative level of what needs to be resolved in relationship.

Practicing Awakened Relating

John and Christiane: Not Believing the Story

John and Christiane met in a spiritual community and have been together since 1989. They both bring a great deal of psychological, emotional, and spiritual maturity to their relationship. In addition to their shared understanding and commitment to the essential truth, John and Christiane also utilize methods that help them to stay awake together. One method they use to resolve conflict is "The Work" of Byron Katie (2002), which is a way of identifying and questioning the thoughts and stories that create separation and suffering so the mind can be allowed to return to its awakened, peaceful nature. Here is a conversation I had with them about their experience with awakened relating.

LML: Each human being is so unique. We each carry our own bundle of conditioning and personality that makes up our individual expression in the world. When two human beings come together, reactions to these differences are inevitable. Please share how you help each other stay awake in the emotional reactions that may arise in relationship because of your differences.

John: First of all, we experience a resonance in silence together that feels natural. It is about just emphasizing the awareness in all experience. Whatever reaction or response we may be having to one another, we can also usually get in touch with the sense of a shared silent awareness at a deeper level. This brings a feeling of space to whatever we are experiencing.

In addition to emphasizing the awareness in all experience, one tool we use is Byron's Katie's inquiry process. If one of us is in a reaction, there is willingness to slow down to sense and feel what is going on, take a look at that, and then see what the projection is. We do this process informally together or with our selves.

Christiane: For me, it is sharing the story of the reaction as it is with no need to change it. We share it knowing it is a story, but giving it the full blast of reality at the same time. We allow it with all the feelings and intensity, without trying to be nice or change it—knowing that it is just a story and not an absolute truth. Once the story is shared with all the feelings that go with it, we can inquire into the belief that generated the reaction. We do the same for the other by listening to their story fully as it is. Then we do Byron Katie's (2002) "Work," which includes asking, "Who would we be without that story?" Asking this question reminds me in a very simple way that there is space in me to welcome life *as it is*, without my stories about it. An alignment with that space naturally happens allowing a detachment from the charge of the story. Doing so in the presence of the other allows us to share the unleashing of energy that was bound up in the story.

John: I think what is important is the willingness to feel, and really be vulnerable, rather than just staying on a cognitive level. It's important to be shaky and in "not knowing" to really be in reaction.

Christiane: For me, fully allowing the entire spectrum of the reaction is Love. When there is this quality of listening, there is a flow even during a reaction. I am willing to let the reaction be, knowing that it isn't who I am. Because of this, it is different from venting. There is a friendly feeling toward the reaction in letting it be and a friendly feeling towards John for being willing to listen. All of this allows for the experience of release and flow.

LML: Yes, it is a certain quality of listening that allows the reaction to be fully expressed and heard without getting caught up in it.

John: That is a key point. This is where the interaction is different than conventional interactions. There is a quality of listening, a quality of openness, and a willingness to let it be and let oneself be without the need to control or manipulate the experience in any way. In addition to vulnerability, there is a trust. There is a trust in the truth and a devotion to truth that we both share. This informs the quality of listening and openness to share and speak the truth. We are willing to see where an honest exploration of the facts will lead, trusting in a deeper unfolding of life—one that is not in our control.

LML: You trust that speaking and allowing the truth on a relative level will naturally lead to a deeper, all-inclusive truth.

Christiane: Yes, that's right. This involves being with what is in the moment, whether pleasant or unpleasant. Emotional reactions that happen in relationship can be considered "unpleasant," but it is a movement of Love to welcome them as much as pleasant experiences.

John: It is facing a difficult situation together and trusting the unfolding. An example of this in our relationship is when Christiane left for France for nine months. She needed to do this to complete her requirements for a retirement pension. There was a knowing that we were not truly separate on an essential level, even though we were so far away from each other.

Christiane: Not being physically together each day allowed us to appreciate each other more. I felt much more concretely that the presence did not need to be physical. He did not need to be there for me to feel the essential connection we have. That contact is much more beyond the physical contact. This was a real learning experience for me. It was a teaching that relationship is far beyond having the person there physically. There was a real sense of that.

John:	There was a clarification of the nonobjective nature of the relationship. Shared presence isn't about space and time. Often when there is a separation, there can be a feeling of lack in some way. But that did not happen for either one of us. We both sensed an inherent fullness. We also felt our own autonomy. There is the essential connection and also a sense of autonomy and freedom. This essential connection is different than merging. It comes with autonomy.

LML:	The essential connection is not dependent on anything.

John:	It is not dependent on anything. That is the beauty of this kind of experience. And, we share natural human feelings of gratitude and reconnection along with this quieter experience of a shared presence.

Christiane:	This experience of shared presence gives a sense of freedom and space for allowing differences. We are extremely different people. We are very different. And, there is room for that.

John:	The underlying sense of autonomy and freedom makes the differences not only okay, but enjoyable. We can truly celebrate our differences.

LML:	And allow each other to be as you are.

John:	Yes, we don't need to manipulate or control each other in any way for us to feel secure. This gives us freedom to love. The question of safety and love, which are so much a part of relationships, changes with this freedom. There is a quality that I haven't mentioned so far, which is an openheartedness that is felt here at the heart center—a felt-sense of openness and allowing.

Christiane: Also, a sense of humor helps a lot!

John: Yes, I think it is an important point to not take ourselves too seriously. Sometimes we get caught in our roles and identities and we can point it out with humor. Again, the understanding that we are not any story that we take ourselves to be allows for space around stories as they may temporarily arise. We don't have to take getting caught seriously. We can laugh at it and let it go.

LML: This is how we can help each other—by staying awake in that understanding and reminding each other, with love and humor, if the understanding appears to be temporarily lost.

John: When both partners are dedicated to their true nature, to being Love, the process accelerates significantly. We both have blind spots, but because of this dedication, we really look carefully at our holding places as they arise.

LML: Awakened relating is a commitment to make living as our true nature the priority in relationship.

John: The commitment is much more than to one another. It is really a commitment to living truth. That's a more fundamental commitment.

Christiane: What feels to me to be the most consistent in our relationship and in my life is this openness; the willingness to be with the unknown moment to moment. This is where I find consistency and substance. There are no boundaries there. There is no person there. When we are together, there is a sense of sharing that openness. In that openness, who are we? We are not a man or a woman there. There is a beauty of the sharing when there is this sense of oneness. And, it's not two people becoming one. It's sharing the oneness that has always been here.

LML: The openness is what is constant and never changing, and the playing out of two personalities and bodies relating together happens within that.

John: There is a knowing of the infinite space in which everything is appearing and disappearing. That's the ground. That feels like the deepest truth. There is a sense of being both in and out of the world. There is that feeling of both witnessing and intimately participating: a spacious intimacy. It is an intimate engagement with a sense of Love and delight, and at the same time it is an openness or vastness that is unbounded and infinite, which is not personal. We could call it a non-personal intimacy that feels very palpable and alive. This intimacy is not just with Christiane; it's an intimacy with all of life.

LML: The true, unbounded Love cannot be confined to one person.

John: No, it can't. However, there are relative boundaries. There is a respect of the human relationship and marriage. Yet, the intimacy is not limited to that. The intimacy is actually not just with people. It is with everything. That understanding feels like it just keeps deepening. The heart just keeps opening and feels more and more gratitude, just for being—for no reason at all.

MEDITATIVE INQUIRY:
Waking Up to Our Stories

An important aspect of staying awake together is to not believe the stories we create about each other, our self, and the relationship. I invite you to look at the stories that your conditioned mind creates. Pay attention and see if you can find at least one story each day that you have believed to be true about yourself or your partner.

Examples of stories about our partner (or other close relationships) are: "They are always _____," or "They are never _____," or "They should _____." (You can fill in the blanks for your specific stories.) If there is an "always," "never," or "should" involved, whether it is about our self or others, that is a big clue that an imaginary story is being created. Once we become aware of the story, we can inquire into it with your awareness and see if there is any truth to it. Ask, "Can I really know that is true?"

One suggestion is to write the story down exactly as your mind is telling it to you and then read it out loud to yourself. What fixed conclusion have you come to about your partner? Please know that all fixed conclusions come from the conceptual mind, never from open awareness. The mind only thinks what it is taught or programmed to think. Therefore, these thought-stories are never the living truth in the moment. Hearing our story read out loud may be enough to expose its illusory nature.

If it still feels true, see if you can find the origins of the story. Take the focus off your partner and back to yourself. Inquire into the aspects of your conditioning or wounding that are at the source of the story. Notice and be present with the emotional charge and the sensations in the body that the story produces. This can lead you to its origins, which you can then allow in present awareness.

As the story loosens its grip, try shifting your attention from the thought-story to the witnessing awareness and rest as that. Let the thoughts go and then see what happens to the story. Notice that the impersonal awareness is not caught up in the story and can see both the story and the sense of separate self it creates. In a moment of falling out of thought and resting into awareness, both the story and the sense of separate self completely dissolves. So, how real is it?

CHAPTER 11

A Love That Knows No Other

True Intimacy

Real love is the One celebrating itself as two.

—Ram Dass

There is nothing more intimate than directly knowing that we are one Being and consciously sharing that together. This oneness is the heart of awakened relating. It is the truest intimacy. It is an intimacy with all beings and all of life. Even though we all long for this intimate union, we are unable to find any lasting experience of it through relationship or sexuality that is based in separation. The paradox is that we are already one Being, and yet, because we don't recognize this, we seek to create union and wholeness in intimate relationship. As David Richo (2002) points out, "We strive for intimacy with the whole universe, not just with one person. We cannot expect from a partner what can only come from the Self/universe/higher power." True intimacy is our natural relationship to reality as it truly is. Every relationship is the One intimately relating with itself.

The Nondual Nature of Awakened Relating

To the rational mind, any discussion of nonduality sounds paradoxical and confusing. Nonduality can never be fully understood by the dualistic mind. It can only be known through direct experience of that which is beyond the mind's reach. If we hope to experience nonduality, it is best to relax the mind and drop into the heart, allowing a non-conceptual *felt sense* of nonduality to emerge from the silence of Being, where true understanding can be found.

I use the word nonduality to mean that the basis or fundamental ground of all the diversity of life is the same and nothing is separate from this ground. Like heat and fire, wet and water, and the sun and its rays, the entire phenomenal world of experience is inseparable from its nondual ground of aware Being. The more we know the Oneness, the more we can fully allow and appreciate the diversity of experience. The global emergence of this fundamental understanding has the potential to significantly change our world and save the human race from the destruction it seems to be barreling toward. So many of the problems in this world are based in our inability to accept our obvious differences because we are not yet seeing our underlying sameness and unity.

Zen Buddhism speaks of "intimacy with the 10,000 things," which means intimacy with everything. We are intimate with everything when we rest in the openness of our Being and fully embrace all that arises. Then, everything is intimately touched by the Love of our true heart. We come to know this Undivided Love through accepting things as they are. Resistance to what is occurring moment to moment is what creates all division. From our conditioned perspective of separation, some experiences are acceptable and some are not, some experiences are intimate and some are not. From the perspective of our undivided nature, all experience is equally intimate and fully embraced; the entire universe is our intimate companion. This understanding is a radical departure from the limited, conventional idea that intimacy is limited to one or a few people.

True intimacy is not an experience, it is our nature, which is open-hearted and all-inclusive. True intimacy is a Love that knows no other. When we let go of our labels and ideas, the beauty of the sacred mystery can come forward in our experience and live consciously through us. Where this sacred mystery most loves to dance is in relationship. This dance of true intimacy is a flow that is exquisitely beautiful and deeply nourishing when it is a free expression of Undivided Love.

Fear of Intimacy

A common problem that people have in relationship is a fear of intimacy. Why do so many of us fear intimacy? On a psychological level, it appears to arise from our conditioning. If we were neglected or hurt by our primary caretakers as open, vulnerable children, then it makes sense that we would fear intimacy when getting close to lovers as an adult. Intimacy requires us to be vulnerable, without the need to defend anything. If it has never been made safe for us to experience this vulnerability, then we feel frightened and we may keep our heart closed to intimacy, rather than risk being hurt again. Yet all the ways we defend and protect ourselves only serve to take us farther away from the intimacy we crave. The longing for intimacy is a natural part of our human experience because, in truth, we are all intimately connected and we all long to come home to this natural union. No matter how great the fear, it is possible to find our way home to true intimacy with openness and courage.

On a more primal level, we fear the dissolution of the familiar sense of a separate self that occurs as we awaken to our undivided nature. If our separate identity is all we have known, we fear the true intimacy of blending with the vast unity of all life. This primal fear is mostly unconscious. It is an anticipatory mental construct that is not based in the direct experience of what true intimacy is. True intimacy involves a willingness to open to this fear and face it, along with all the pain and hurt that formed the foundation upon which fear uneasily rests. Meeting the fear directly in the accepting space of pure awareness allows us to move through it and touch the underlying intimacy of Being. Through repeated experiences of this sacred meeting, we become familiar with how safe and nourishing true intimacy is and we develop the trust to let go of separation. The dissolution of separation *is* intimacy, in the truest sense.

We Are Both Human and Divine

True intimacy is the marriage of our human and divine natures. Another way of saying this is that the relative and absolute come together as two expressions of the same one reality. These two aspects of reality are equal and complimentary aspects of the same, singular truth. As the Buddha's Heart Sutra (Tanahashi 2016) tells us, "Form is emptiness and emptiness is form." Even though our unlimited, divine nature is always present, it is possible to overlook it and live as though we only have a limited, human nature.

The deepest offering of intimate relationship is to teach us how to embody our divine nature in our humanity. Our discomfort and dissatisfaction let us know when we are not allowing both natures to be revealed in their natural union. If we pay attention, it doesn't take long before it becomes painfully apparent that relating only from our conditioned human nature cannot keep true Love alive in a relationship. And, if we relate only from spiritual concepts or from temporary transcendent states, we are bypassing our humanness, which must be included in order for awakened relating to flower.

Awakened relating involves staying present with both; learning to solidly rest in our shared Being while relating and being present with what arises in our humanness. True intimacy is a meeting at the juncture of the absolute and relative expressions of reality. We meet at this juncture by fully embracing relative reality while maintaining conscious contact with the unifying field of awareness in which it is all appearing. This unconditional allowing is what dissolves the sense of separation and brings us into true intimacy. We come into the fullness of our divine nature through fully embracing our human nature.

In the following conversations, I asked spiritual teachers Rupert, Adayshanti, and Mukti to elaborate more on what I am referring to as true intimacy from their deep understanding of the nondual nature of intimacy.

Rupert: Intimacy Is the Dissolution of Separation

Rupert teaches that if the fundamental truth of reality is that there truly is no separate other, there can be no relationship in the conventional sense of the word. Relationship implies an interaction between two, which it is on the relative plane, but that is not all it is. Relationship also has the potential to be a conscious meeting in the one, undivided Being we all share. Remember, in truth, we are always and only relating to our other Self. Rupert discusses this radical truth and how it can bring human beings into more harmonious relating with one another. He points to true intimacy as the dissolution of boundaries, of all that creates an imaginary limitation and division between us.

LML: There is a lot of confusion about what intimacy really means. Can you talk about what it means, in the truest sense, to be intimate in relationship and in life?

Rupert: To be intimate with someone or something means not to have a distance or a boundary between oneself and that person or object—the dividing line that apparently separates one from the person or object dissolves. For that dividing line to dissolve, everything that defines our self as a finite subject, and correspondingly, everything that defines the other as a finite object must dissolve or, more accurately, be seen to be nonexistent.

In other words, the apparently finite forms of our self and the other must dissolve or be seen as nonexistent or imaginary. It is those limitations in our self, and the corresponding limitations in the other, that keep our self and the other from being intimate—from touching each other, from being close. So, what is it that prevents intimacy? What is the line between the me and the you? What is that line made of? Whatever that line is made of is what separates the two, the self and the other, the me and the you.

Two bodies can obviously never be truly intimate, because there is a dividing line between them. Even if they are touching each other, even if they are totally wrapped up in each other, they are still two finite, limited bodies. However close or entwined those bodies become, they never become truly intimate because they never cease to be two bodies; they never lose their limitations. No matter how hard we try to find true intimacy through merging our body with another body, we can never find it like that.

When two minds meet, that is, when two thoughts meet, or when two series of thought dialogues meet with one another, the boundary that defines the two thoughts is not as clearly defined as the one that divides two bodies. Nevertheless, all thoughts are limited, so there can be no true meeting in the mind. No matter how hard we try to understand one another—even if we share all the same beliefs, interests, and cultural conditioning—there can be no true intimacy in a meeting of minds.

So, in what realm of our experience is it possible to be totally without limits, and therefore without a dividing line between our self and the other? What is it in each of us that is truly without limits and therefore has the potential to truly touch one another, to truly come close, to be one? That is what intimacy is: to lose oneself. To lose oneself means to lose one's sense of limitation, separateness, or otherness. Only that in us that is without limit could possibly be a candidate for true intimacy. What is that? It is the presence of awareness—just our innate, aware Being. To look for intimacy anywhere else is a source of conflict. It is doomed to fail. It is for that reason that so many relationships start out promising, but fall apart.

Everyone longs for true intimacy, which means the loss of boundaries, the loss of that which defines us and makes it seem as if we are something that is temporary and limited. We have a deep conditioning in our culture that merging with a person physically will bring about this loss of everything that defines us. That is why the desire for sexual union is so closely allied to our desire for intimacy. In fact, in most people, it is mixed up. For most people, the impulse to unite physically with another is the highest candidate for this experience of intimacy. Indeed, when we come close to another in sexual intimacy there *is* a temporary loss of limitation and separation. There is a kind of merging or melting of one's sense of being a separate self, and a dis-solving of the sense of a separate other. And, in that merging, we taste the true intimacy.

What is really happening in this experience is that all the beliefs, and more importantly, the *feelings* of being temporary, finite, and limited are dissolved, and as a result, we are plunged into our true nature of unlimited, open awareness. That is the experience of true intimacy, which means lack of limits, lack of otherness. Our true nature is unlimited; there is no otherness. It can never experience something other than itself, unless it imagines it is a temporary and finite self. Only as a temporary and finite self can we experience some-thing other than our self. Thus, we have to overlook the knowing of our own Being in order to experience another. As soon as we overlook the knowing of our own unlimited Being, which cannot know another, we lose the sense of limitlessness, the sense of total openness, and the total lack of resistance to all experience. We become, or seem to become, a finite self. The first desire that this finite self has is to return again to the intimacy, the openness, and the Love that it once knew. Thus, the desire for intimacy in relationship is the apparently separate self's desire to be divested of its own limitations.

The ultimate intimacy is where we never know anything other than our self. It is not about intimacy with one person, although many of us first taste it with one person. But in time, that intimacy expands beyond the relationship with one person. It expands until it includes everyone and everything. It is expressed in one particular way with an intimate partner, but it is exactly the same intimacy that is expressed in a glance at a homeless person on the street, or when we pay a cab driver and look him in the eye and say, "Thank you." It is the same intimacy that is being shared and expressed in appropriate ways with everyone.

LML: For many people, there is resistance to letting go of the "spe-cialness" of the Love that is shared in a romantic relationship. They may feel that something will be lost if there is Love for all beings.

Rupert: There is still a unique and special way in which we share this Love with our intimate partner. It's just that the Love is no longer portioned out. We don't give a certain amount to one person and nothing to another. Love cannot be portioned out in this way.

In fact, it is impossible to love a person, because a person, as such, is finite. In order to know a finite object, let alone love a finite object, we first have to believe and feel our self to be a finite subject. And, to conceive of our self as a finite subject, we have to overlook the knowing of our own Being as it truly is. In other words, we have to forget our self. We have to cease knowing our own Being as it truly is. Only a separate self knows a separate other, and then loves some of those separate others and not others. So, it's actually not possible to love another as a separate self.

LML: We do not actually love the "other," because we are really only loving different expressions of our Self.

Rupert: Yes, Love is not a special kind of relationship. It is the dissolution of relationship, the dissolution of self and other. Relationship is always between two. True Love is the end of relationship between two separate selves, although this Love is expressed in and as relationship. This truth is not just for a rarified few anymore. Our world culture can no longer afford to ignore it.

Practicing Awakened Relating

Adyashanti and Mukti: The Paradox of True Intimacy

In the following conversation, Adyashanti (Adya) and his wife Mukti explored the paradox of true intimacy and awakened relating with my husband John (JLW) and me (LML). The deepest truth of relationship includes the truth that we are one Being relating as two very different expressions of itself. Adya and Mukti's share their lived experience of being in relationship with a profound understanding of this paradox.

LML: I'd like to begin this discussion on true intimacy with a quote from you Adya (1999): "Inherent within the revelation of perfect unity is the realization that there is no other. The implications of this realization reveal that in order to manifest that unity in the relative world, one must renounce the dream of being a separate self-seeking to obtain anything through relationship with another." That pretty much summarizes what I am trying to say in this book. Can you say more about that?

Adya: What comes up for me is that any truth always seems to live in some sort of an amazing paradox. There is the paradox of no other and the fact that anybody who has been in relationship also experiences two very unique, autonomous individuals. The truth of that is that just because you have two unique, autonomous individuals, doesn't mean that you have separation. It doesn't mean that you have some ultimate state of otherness. In the more relative sense, however, what we are often in relationship with is not an absolute otherness, but we are almost always relating to a relative otherness in the sense of difference—difference of ideas, opinion, taste, preference—all sorts of difference. This is the way that what we call "the One" operates in a unique, autonomous way. To me, that's the dance of sacred relationship.

LML: Why is it that so many people who have had some awakening or have realized to some degree that there is no other still have such a difficult time with relationship?

Adya: Just because you have realized that doesn't mean that all of a sudden—*boom*—you are great at relationship. Some people can have a deep experience of no otherness and be a complete disaster in relationship. People can have an experience of total separation and also be a complete disaster at relationship. Obviously, no otherness is a really important component, but it doesn't suddenly make everything work right. There is some other dynamic that I think is also at play.

For me, relationship is about flow; it's two different people interacting with each other. Sometimes when people have an experience of no otherness, they can kind of get stuck in that and they don't really know what it's like to flow together. I think that is one of the reasons why some people who have deep experiences of unity sometimes don't know how to relate well. Some people go into relationship and to their surprise, their own wounding that they were certain was no longer there is brought to the fore. They can be upset by that, they can be angered by that, they can be saddened by that, and they can be confused by that. I think a lot of people harbor the idea that an experience of unity will cause all of their relational issues to sort of disappear. Although I think that some fundamental relational issues do get resolved with the realization of no other.

LML: Can you give an example of what may get resolved through realization?

Adya: In my experience, what fell away with awakening that directly affects the quality of relating was being attached to my point of view. Which meant that I could listen much better and not filter what was being said to me through the filter of my ego. Making any sort of emotional demands on people also fell away. I was no longer looking to be fulfilled through or by anyone, which paradoxically makes being together much more enjoyable. There were many other changes that occurred, but these are the ones that stand out most. The result of these changes was that I now experience everyone as an aspect of myself. It's a profound sense of spiritual intimacy that never wavers.

JLW: It seems to me that it is a process of embodying the realization of no other as related to our partner.

Adya: Yes, yes. I think it is a really important thing that you mention, John. There is the realization or revelation of no other. Then, there is, "How does that trickle down when I have to embody it while relating to somebody?" If the other has a different point of view, can I see that their point of view is also "no other?" That is the ability in the moment to see that someone's very different way of looking at something doesn't mean that creates otherness. In other words, it is like, "The One sees it that way over there." It's still the One. In seeing that, I relate to it in a different way. Then, I have to be in some sort of fluid dance or dynamic. I can't be as oppositional as I might want to be.

JLW: That necessitates an honoring of the apparent other that wouldn't be there otherwise, and an allowing of the differences.

Adya: When you are in separation, it is difficult to allow differences. And, if you are stuck in the revelation of oneness and haven't embodied it, then that can also make it difficult for you to truly honor differences. I often hear people say something like, "Well, I see that everything is One, but my partner is just an unenlightened stone and if he or she could see that, we would get along so much better." They might not say that outright, but you can feel it, and the "no otherness" just breaks down.

LML: It is still another form of something needing to be different than it is, which always causes division.

Adya: Yes, and I like the word that John used: "honoring." It is about honoring differences. Even if you don't agree with them, you can honor them.

JLW: For me, that involves not quite taking myself so seriously and not assuming that I'm right, which, of course, I tend to do.

Adya: Yes. My point of view is just another point of view, one of an infinite number of possibilities. It is difficult to speak about the paradox of this, and certainly difficult to write about. …It's seeing what it's like when two people are holding their point of view lightly, but they haven't abdicated their point of view.

One thing that I think is ironic to the point of being hilarious is that truth is the one thing that can't be stated. We can state no otherness and we can state autonomy or separation, but what you are hinting at is that you can't directly state the truth that embraces the paradox. You can never actually put it into a coherent statement.

LML: It can't be stated, but somehow it can be known. We can only point to that knowing.

Adya: Yes, when we are really listening, somehow, we intuit it. Somehow, we know it, but we can't even tell ourselves. For myself, I can't even tell myself what it is exactly that I know. But, I can intuit it very, very strongly. I can feel it. I can sense it. It is there as obviously as it can be. But, if I try to ask myself, "Okay Adya, what exactly is that truth that you know?" I can't even tell it to myself. Truth is the one thing that you can't say to yourself, and you can't say it to somebody else. You can say things that give a direction, almost like sheep herding. You're herding all the points of view into this place, but once you get them all into this place, you can't really name the place.

Mukti: An image came to me as you have been talking. I was trying to think how someone would respond to this conversation if they had no concept of oneness. I thought of the experience of having a human body and not often thinking that our left hand is different than our right hand. But, if we are doing certain tasks or if we have an injury to one hand or something, and they are not working together in a way that we are used to them working, then we notice the difference. This is one way we might try to convey the notion that there can be an experience of one body with two different parts functioning differently.

JLW: Yes. One body with two different hands is a metaphor for one Being expressing as two different points of view or preferences.

LML: Do either of you have a story or example of being together in relationship with an understanding of unity?

Mukti: I can't think of an example of big importance, but I can think of a little one. One example is when we just have different preferences. When one of us has been resting for a number of days and the other person comes back from having worked for a couple of days and is tired. Then, we are in different rhythms. So, let's say that Adya has been home and he is ready to play and says, "Let's go to the movies! Let's go adventure." And, I am feeling the exact opposite and want to just hole up and not do anything. So, at times, the rhythms and preferences are different.

LML: How does that play out—within the context of the understanding that we are speaking of?

Mukti: I'm not sure if this is about the understanding of unity, but how it plays out is that the more important need rules in the moment. It just becomes obvious who has the greater need and that becomes the ruling factor. I think that has to do with the care we have for each other and the relationship. The wellbeing of the other is the higher priority. Sometimes I am very tired and I will go to the movie anyway because I know that will bring Adya a lot of joy. Other times, I am way too tired and I just can't do it. Then, he is so happy that I say that and am taking care of myself, which is the higher priority in that case. It works out when each person is looking after the highest wellbeing of both themselves and the other.

Adya: Even with a minor difference, like the one Mukti is talking about, in almost every situation where there is a difference of preference or experience, almost always one of us has something that is more essential and is not just a surface desire. I think that the unity part comes in because it helps us to stay connected to what is important and really rules in that moment. You are not looking from such a personal place; you are looking out for the other.

Mukti: Even in the example I gave where maybe I am too tired because I have been on a long trip or something, I really value the closeness of the relationship, so that is the higher value in that example. But, then in another moment where I feel like I just can't do it, I am really valuing health and wellbeing, which potentially supports the relationship as well. When we take care of ourselves, then we can be present with the other the next day when we are rested.

LML: To me, that comes back to what we were previously talking about in terms of telling the truth. In an ultimate sense, we can't really tell the truth, but we can be with what's true in the moment if we are not holding on to it, needing it to be any particular way.

Adya: I think there is a relational truth that comes about when you have two people, who, in our case, are really committed to what the truth of the moment is. Then, there's often a third thing that comes into the room. I might have an idea and Mukti might have an idea, but if we dialogue in a creative way that is not attached to our own point of view, often there is a third point of view that comes into being in a moment of relating this way. Both people will notice it when that arises. It will be, "Oh, that's it." That's the thing that neither one of us really brought to the table, but came about because we were relating in a way that was open to something else becoming obvious. This also happens in discussions at our sangha office. Some resolution or solution shows up that doesn't really belong to anybody. It is the gestalt of the moment that brings it forward. Everybody recognizes it when that happens.

JLW: This happens when we write together. When the two of us are working together, we'll find some sentence or idea that neither of us feels is quite right. And, if we are not holding onto a point of view and can just relax into stillness and talk about it, then something emerges that comes through both of us and we both go, "Oh! That's it!"

Adya: That's it exactly, John. You both recognize it, right? I think that's kind of like magic.

LML: And, that arises out of the shared commitment to truth.

Adya: Yeah, shared commitment to truth and it also goes back to the theme of your book—a deeper sense of unity. When we have that deeper sense of unity, it makes it a lot easier to either relinquish or hold our own position lightly.

Mukti: Adya and I often have a conversation about what might be the best solution or resolution; what is best for the whole. For example, I am working on a retreat policy and we're balancing different factors where we are trying to meet the needs of various people and we don't quite have the right solution. But, as we talk about it, something that we haven't even thought of before appears that somehow seems to take care of all the people we've been considering. It has that flavor of serving the whole.

Adya needs to *see* something more concretely; and I can work things out more in my head, visualizing. Recognition of the most obvious thing can happen when we are trying to put something together or trying to do something aesthetic. When we actually have it mocked up and all the parts are in place, we just know if it works or it doesn't. It's like you know when the ingredients you are cooking with taste good or they don't. Sometimes we could be disagreeing and as soon as we get it into a concrete state, it resolves.

LML: So, in summary, when we are awake in our relating, to whatever degree is possible in the moment, we stay connected and we are open and collaboratively creative together. We learn to work things out in ways that meet everyone's needs and don't end up feeling like we had to forsake ourselves to compromise or keep the peace. When we are centered in ourselves, we know the source of satisfaction, well-being, and Love is within us. We aren't off balance, trying to push or pull the other so they'll align with our point of view. True intimacy allows us to hold our point of view more lightly and consider theirs more openly.

Adya: That's beautiful. A great definition of unity is an absolute intimacy with all things. Inherent in the experience of unity is the experience of great intimacy and great Love and care. In terms of relationship, it's a balanced view between the One and the many. True unity includes, but also transcends differentiation. Love is unity in action.

MEDITATIVE INQUIRY:
Gazing into Oneness Together

The following meditation is adapted with permission from the group work of spiritual teacher Sperry Andrews. This gazing meditation is a powerful and direct way to practice awakened relating and experience the true intimacy of shared Being together.

Sit facing each other and spend some time meditating on the breath with eyes closed to quiet and calm the mind. When you are ready, open your eyes and simply rest your attention on the eyes you are looking at with a soft, wide-angle gaze. Notice the field of undivided attention that opens up in you and between the two of you. As you relax in this field together, it may become palpable as a presence of love, stillness, silence, or peace. Allow those qualities to arise as you pay attention to what is within yourself and within the eyes of the other. Notice that what is looking is not divided. It accepts everything equally. Be aware of being aware, together. See directly that it is the same awareness looking out of your eyes that is also looking out of the eyes of your other Self. Bask in the direct experience of this shared unity.

As you continue gazing, take turns speaking your direct experience in the immediate moment. Use just one or a few words to describes your experience such as, "openness," "stillness," "unconditional acceptance, or "no separation." This keeps you grounded in relationship, the body, and the here and now, while relaxing into what is formless and changeless. As you continue gazing and sharing, the focus naturally shifts from the content (words and meaning) to the context of your combined wakefulness. In this way, you are practicing awakened relating by staying awake to shared Being while relating.

This is a powerful practice for couples to do regularly, as it deepens the direct experience of Undivided Love, which is true intimacy. It can also be used any time you become lost in the stories and dramas of the mind together. Even a few minutes of gazing will bring you back to the sanity and clarity of Love. It is also healing to do this practice with yourself in a mirror, allowing any self-negativity to be dissolved in the Love of Self recognition.

CHAPTER 12

Love in Action
Changing Our World
Through Awakened Relating

*If a couple wants to be truly happy, they have to be serving something
larger than themselves, even larger than their relationship.*

—Adyashanti

It is the natural impulse of Love, and therefore our nature, to be of
benefit to others. We may not see it in the conditioned behaviors of
many human beings, but we are all naturally altruistic. Inherent in our
Being is an uncontrived compassion that arises naturally as our sense
of separation dissolves. All of creation is held in the heart of great
compassion. There is a capacity in each of us to connect with our
inherently altruistic nature and be of benefit to others. When we
operate from wholeness and from Undivided Love, we are spontaneously being of the most benefit.

Once we come to recognize our beneficial nature, we have the
choice, moment to moment, to live as that or to live as the imaginary
ego-self. These are two very different ways of being and relating in life.
The ego-self is not focused on benefitting others. In fact, it's just the
opposite. The ego is primarily concerned with itself and what it can
get from others, since it is simply a survival mechanism. Even if it is
doing good deeds, there is always an element of self-gratification and
self-aggrandizement because it attaches a sense of self to these actions.

I used to feel so ashamed of how self-centered my ego was until I realized that it is the nature of all egos and it is not the truth of who I am. The more out of touch we are with our true nature, the tighter the ego holds on to its self-centered survival strategies. In its ignorance of our compassionate nature, the ego gets lost in a dream of perceived lack, which results in fear and selfishness.

When the ego-self is out of control and spins vast webs of distorted power, it can become monstrous in its greed and disconnectedness. This is evidenced by the current state of our world. According to the World Food Programme (2017), approximately 815 million people do not have enough food to eat, with 98 percent of them living in developing countries. That is one in nine people on Earth. There is not a shortage of food; this situation has been created by exploitative greed that arises out of a lack of *felt* connection with the whole.

Wealth is being concentrated into the hands of fewer and fewer to the detriment of the majority. Solutions to many environmental, social, economic, and medical issues are either not allowed, sidelined, or eliminated when they cut into corporate profits. This exemplifies the extremes to which the self-serving, fear-based, separate self can go. The focus on short-term gains and the failure to address the long-term consequences of this is now risking the survival of life on this planet. A more inclusive awakened relating that includes a compassionate caring for all beings as our other Self is now needed more than ever.

The apparent separate self has been allowed to dominate our body-heart-mind and world with its confusion and distorted perspective on reality. It takes tremendous courage to stand up to the domination of the fear-based mind, within ourselves, our relationships, and in the world around us. Each time we say *yes* to Undivided Love, we are saying *no* to this domination, which has become increasingly destructive in our world. Each one of us who takes this stand is greatly influencing the whole in a powerful way and is creating far-reaching ripples in the field of human consciousness. The courage to stand in truth, no matter what, is an honoring of the essence of all life on behalf of all beings.

Undivided Love in Action

The conditioned mind responds to the imbalances in the world with despair, anger, and fear. When we know our undivided nature, we can simultaneously hold the suffering of the world *and* the truth that in the core of our Being, *all is well*. From the vantage point of Undivided Love, we experience the paradox of both unconditional acceptance of what is and a sacred outrage at the unnecessary suffering of our other Selves as result of greed and ignorance. This sacred outrage is coming from an all-powerful Love that is not passive. It is a fierce Love that comes from wisdom and compassion. The Love in action that is being called forth today is a Love born of the same outrage that a mother would feel if she saw her child being harmed. She does not just accept what is happening without taking action. Action is required and it comes from Love.

Knowing the deeper truth that *all is well* makes it possible to truly face what is happening without avoiding it or getting stuck in the polarized duality of "us versus them." Then, we are available to address the imbalances in ways that will be most beneficial. This is how we can relate to our world in a more awakened way, which I see as a radical political act. It is an undivided and awakened activism that will allow our greater intelligence to transform our ailing world and provide the inclusive solutions to the critical problems we are all now facing.

Awakened Activism

The higher purpose of relationship is to awaken consciousness and then to be a beneficial offering to the world. As couples awaken together, they create a force of Love that reaches beyond the couple. There is a vast and largely untapped power in two or more coming together as Undivided Love. The consciously united Being of the couple becomes a beneficial power in the world. No longer needing to "get" from each other, the Love and compassion inherent in our nature overflows to others. All the energy that was previously spent on conflicts, blaming, and endlessly processing relationship "issues" can now be expressed through being of service. It is also true that at any stage of relationship development, we can become more in touch with our compassionate nature through being of service to each other, to our community, and the world. As Mahatma Gandhi allegedly said, "The best way to find yourself is to lose yourself in the service of others."

We don't have to wait to be fully awake or embodied to be of service. In fact, awakening is an ongoing unfolding for everyone. No matter where we are on the path, we can put our devotion to awakened Love into action in small ways every day by simply being open to how Love wants to move. It could be anything from little acts of kindness to organizing a global movement, and anything in between. Practicing Love in action brings us closer to our naturally compassionate, altruistic nature. The more we *be* that, the more naturally beneficial we become. On a path of awakening, I believe that being of service to our other Selves is as important as meditation.

When awakened relating extends beyond the couple, they become one movement of awakened activism. This could involve social, political action, but is not limited to that. Each one of us, and each couple, has a unique gift to offer the world. It could be Love in action as a teacher, a doctor, a gardener, a parent, or in countless other ways that Love can move through us. It doesn't matter what it is. What matters is that the action is naturally flowing freely from the source of Love and wisdom. Awakened activism is Undivided Love in action. I would like to share an example of a couple whose relationship has blossomed into awakened activism that involves social and political work.

Margo and John: Awakened Couples Activism

Margo and John have been committed to awakened relating throughout their relationship, which began in 1983 and has grown to include what they refer to as "awakened couple's activism." As they say, "From the beginning, our relationship was focused on supporting awakening for self, other, community, and the world." Together, they have helped seed and grow initiatives that are addressing environmental, social, political, economic, and spiritual challenges that we face in our world today. This is part of a conversation I had with them about awakened couple's activism.

LML: I want to discuss what I see as the heart of who you are as a couple, which is living the deepest truth, both in your relationship and in the world.

John: An integral part of our relationship is an ever-present calling to be of service. In my thirties, I recognized this as the motivating factor in my life. There is nothing I did to cause it. It always felt like grace. The call to be of benefit is a moment to moment arising in the field of Being. It is always present. It is a remarkable gift. Margo and I have been very fortunate to have that in common. And, whether we are working solo or together, we carry the vibrational heart-wisdom of the one shared essence that we are.

Margo: Yes, one way we have followed the calling to serve has been to demystify enlightenment in everyday life. Our species has a large case of mistaken identity. It is becoming globally recognized that to live from the true nature of mind, our natural state, is the common heritage and birthright for all humanity. It is not special. It is ordinary and accessible. That is such an important part of what your book is about—the democratizing of waking up individually, as couples, families, communities, and the world. The simple and direct instructions that you give for demystifying awakening, which are presented so beautifully in your book, become a perfect training manual for awakened activism.

As this plays out in our lives, we're in ongoing awe and gratitude as the field of infinite intelligence allows wisdom, love, skillful means, and natural ethics to arise as needed in our relationship or in any realm that we're a part of. As a couple, or for any collective, when awakened awareness is the central operating principle, rather than the separate self, then optimal solutions can creatively arise beyond the conventions of time, space, and causality. Those solutions will always be for the benefit of all, which includes oneself. Since we are each expressions of the all, and because our work flows out of this understanding, we are lighter, have more fun, and collaborate more easily. We don't take our points of view so seriously as they arise, especially those that create separation. This is actually the One awareness happily creating with itself!

LML: Could you speak about the current state of the planetary challenges we all find ourselves in? As "awakened activists," how are you addressing these challenges?

Margo: We often refer to the current Earth story as global awakening playing "beat the clock" with mass extinction. We live on a planet on fire! We can start with naming global warming and climate chaos, nuclear proliferation, and then all the interlocking and collapsing systems—political, social, economic, environmental, peacemaking— topped off with population growth and science and technology moving at radical speed with no inherent ethics built in. Yikes! A lot of provocation for waking up! Simultaneously, bright flames of awakening are coming together all over our planet into an emerging bonfire of Oneness.

When we can simultaneously hold the ultimate view of awareness that there is nothing to change or fix, and whatever happens is okay, then more energy, creativity, and solutions become available. This is often a challenging pivot for activists to make. The greatest change is in nothing to change, and simply to relax with everything, just as it is. From that perspective, what spontaneously arises is "awakened activism" and the increasing capacity for indestructible stability under maximum stress. That allows change to be facilitated with creative clarity in ways that otherwise might not happen.

John: There's been another part of the path for me in becoming friends with the rage and fear that is so divisive and prevalent in the field of social and political activism. It was a struggle for me to let those feelings be there when they arose without identifying with them. For a long time after the United States invaded Iraq, I felt a reservoir of rage that I didn't know how to deal with. It was just there every time I checked in. Then one day a friend of ours used a term I had not heard before: "transcendent sorrow." Somehow the rage dissolved into underlying sorrow. I came to know that I could begin to face and feel that sorrow for so much that is going on in our world, without having to change it, not just with Iraq and wars in general, but with the whole range of global, human suffering. Once that sorrow was faced and felt, a new level of compassionate and discerning activism emerged. I was no longer stuck in the rage or underlying fear. I could see myself in all the human characters involved in war and peace, while understanding and loving them, and, at the same time, embracing the natural cycles of creation and destruction, good and bad, dark and light, and so on.

I would also add that when we are being and moving as the One, it allows us to be with and overcome not just our individual fear of death, but also the fear of our species' extinction. As we use the tools found in this book and elsewhere, we can enter into the world with equanimity and fearlessness in the face of great suffering. In awakened activism, we don't respond with fearful urgency. We can respond, as Margo has often said, by "moving at the speed of Love with a relaxed and joyful urgency."

Practicing Awakened Relating

Adyashanti and Mukti: Devotion in Action

Another form of Undivided Love in action is the way it is moving through Adyashanti and Mukti as spiritual teachers. In this continuation of the conversation between Adyashanti (Adya), Mukti, my husband John (JLW), and me (LML), we discuss ways in which their relationship has expanded to be of benefit to many people around the world. Adya and Mukti's spiritual teaching work is making a significant contribution to our world by supporting the awakening of thousands of people. Their relationship also serves as an example of awakened relating for many.

LML: When two come together with a commitment to a deeper truth, we could say that a third thing emerges from that kind of

relating: an intention for the benefit of the whole. When two of us
are focusing this way, it becomes a movement of benefit in the world,
and I see your relationship as being that.

Adya: A lot of it comes down to what a relationship is founded upon.
What is the ultimate glue that holds it together? In Mukti's and my
case, from very early on it was pretty obvious to me that where we
fundamentally meet is in spirit. I know that's a very abstract, esoteric
sounding idea, but for me, it is very concrete. On the exterior, we are
very different. When you take two people like us with the amount of
differences we have, I don't think it would work out well in a lot of
relationships. The reason that it works out so amazingly well for us is
that the place where we fundamentally meet is in spirit, which is really
hard to define.

Some relationships are built around shared interests, hobbies, and
attraction. There's shared experience at the base of how two people
connect. When spirit is the fundamental way that people connect,
they are connecting through something that is very intimate, and, in
that sense, personal, but it also opens up into something bigger. Our
fundamental connection is in spirit and so our participation in the
world is fundamentally spiritual. What holds the relationship together
becomes what you have to offer to the world.

If a couple wants to be truly happy, they have to be serving something larger than themselves, even larger than their relationship. To be
happy, we have to be serving something else, right? This doesn't mean
you have to be on a stage. Even if it is serving a higher ideal, two
people, or a group of people, to be happy and functional, we have to be
serving something bigger.

LML: This is true because it is our nature to be compassionate and
engaged in serving others. Love naturally moves in this way.

Adya: Yes. There has to be an avenue through which that Love
moves. And, sometimes on a personal level, that's really nice and
enriching. It's satisfying and sometimes it's challenging. The nice thing

is that it doesn't really matter if it is challenging, almost anything that is worthwhile in life is challenging.

LML: Even if it is challenging, Love will find its way. On the other hand, relationship in separation tends to be focused on self-concern. It's about what I can get from you or what I need from you. There can be too much focus on each other. If we don't need to get our needs met by our partner, then Love can move in a bigger way in the world.

Adya: I think that's really a fundamentally important way to put it, Lynn Marie. The other person is not there to meet your needs, even your biggest, most altruistic needs. When we participate in a more compassionate, loving way, partnership can be a platform from which compassionate action can really flower. And, of course, that compassionate way of being in the world comes back to the relationship because it is enriching for the relationship. If the relationship is too focused in on itself, if we're focusing toward each other too much, then we're bound to be in discord and conflict because nobody can give the other person everything; it's just impossible. In our culture, we are talking about relationship in terms of, "What can you give me?" Of course, in a personal relationship or even a friendship, it has to be satisfying and enriching, but if it is based upon what that person can do for you, you are bound for trouble.

Ultimately, it goes back to something you are writing about, Lynn Marie, which is that we can't actually get Love from another person. In fact, my experience is that every amount of Love that we experience is a Love that is coming from within us. The Love that is inside you is evoked. And, so, I love you and I appreciate you for being able to evoke that within me, but we don't have to go and get Love from somebody else and take it into ourselves. We can experience somebody else's love, but as long as the reference is outside of us, it's never enough. There are a lot of people who have been profoundly, deeply loved by someone else and they are still miserable.

LML: To me, that's because they haven't really contacted their fundamental nature, which is essentially Love.

Adya: Yes, I think so. I think that what's happening to us all the time. All the states we experience—love, hatred, jealousy, happiness, joy—are being evoked within us, rather than being sourced from the outside. Recognizing the source as an idea can be interesting, but as an actual lived experience, it is life changing.

LML: When we first met both of you in 1997, Mukti was not yet teaching and there were just a handful of people attending meetings with Adya. Now, you are both teaching and you are reaching thousands of people together. Is there is anything you'd like to share about that apparent evolution of your relationship and how it blossomed in that way?

Mukti: Yes, there are actually two different topics there. There is the topic of the relationship being an example for others and the topic of moving beyond it and out into the world. When Adya and I are just being ourselves, there is not necessarily an intention that the way we relate to each other will be attracting a large number of people. But, it happens through example and that example conveys something through a kind of transmission. People have their eyes open for it, they are hungry for it, or they are drinking in the example of sanity and loving relating. And, somehow, when they recognize it, it opens something in them. It opens a possibility. The openness that is created in them can be filled with the same potential within themselves. They can recognize it because there is something within them of that potential, which starts to come alive. Then, they realize how important it is to them and how much they value it. The more they recognize it, the higher priority it becomes.

People have told me that when they think of our relationship, they realize that it is possible. They don't want to sell themselves short any more. They want to aim for something saner, more workable, and more loving. That's a theme that I have heard a lot over the years.

Adya: Our relationship has become more public, in a sense, over the years. We are both out there teaching, so we are away from each other more. In a certain sense, there is a kind of sacrifice to that because we are separated often. But, even though we are making those kinds of sacrifices, the relationship has become bigger and it has enhanced our personal relationship by both of us being involved in work that is bigger than us individually and as a couple, too. This is extremely enriching to our relationship.

Also, as a male teacher, I have had a lot of women over the years mention that they have gotten a lot out of the fact that they can be around me and Mukti and they can just feel our commitment to each other. I think there are a lot of students who have been wounded by very promiscuous teachers—most often men, but not always. Being an example for others is an unintended result of our relationship. Because we are so monogamous (that's just part of our DNA), some people notice that it is possible to be in a position of power and not misuse authority in those ways.

There ultimately isn't such a thing as a private life because our lives affect so many people. Even if we don't have a public place in life, each of our lives affects innumerable people.

JLW: A personal relationship perceived as non-impactful is a delusion. It's not real.

Adya: Yes. It's a delusion, but it is a real leap to really take responsibility for how impactful your life is on others.

JLW: Well, for me, I had to make mistakes interpersonally so I could recognize how impactful my choices are.

Adya: That's how we all go, right? As you've heard me say many times, if we wanted to be perfect, we should never have been born as human beings! But, I do think that we can take responsibility for ourselves. We can hold our integrity, which is totally different than trying to be perfect. Part of being awake is to realize that we actually really don't want to cause harm. It is not any kind of an ideal. You just don't feel like participating in causing harm, if you can avoid it.

Mukti: I would like to mention the importance of devotion. Relationship can bring in an element of devotion to a spiritual path that is largely focused on truth. The example of my relationship with Adya on a larger stage is not only that it has been healing for people who have had difficult pasts with teachers who acted without integrity, but it also offers the transmission of the component of devotion in action, which is a good compliment for the teachings that tend to emphasize truth more than devotion. Real caring and caretaking, respect, honoring, and commitment convey something that reaches people below the mind, below thought, in the heart.

LML: That is a beautiful way to put it, "devotion in action." When we are not looking to the other to be the source of Love, that devotion can truly flower because it is a devotion to something larger than the person, to the essence of Being.

Mukti: It is. Also, as you were saying, it is our nature. It is more about *being* devotion and expression as devotion than being the object of devotion.

LML: As our nature becomes free to express itself, it moves as devotion, love, compassion—that's what it naturally does.

Mukti: Yes. Also, as we express ourselves in that way, the freer we become.

LML: Our world is in great need of having relationship be more of an expression of our true nature.

Adya: That is ultimately what is needed, isn't it? People need to start actually getting along together, but boy is that a big one!

LML: I don't think that human beings can ultimately get along if we are relating from within a belief in division and separation.

Adya: Yes, and I think what is equally important is for people to develop a relatively high degree of emotional maturity. As we have already established, you can have an experience of nonseparation, but you also need emotional maturity, which is what it takes to be in relationship. It takes a deep, profound maturity. Some of that comes with the deep experience of unity and some of it develops in other ways. They are inseparable. You don't get profound relationships based in unity without deep, profound emotional maturity. They are linked together and they need each other to come into expression, but they don't always come as a package deal. I think a lot of spiritual people are disappointed when they discover that they not only have to realize unity, but they also have to emotionally grow up to embody it and express it. So, in the bigger scheme of things, the world does need the experience of unity, and we also need a deep experience of emotional maturity. Both of those are really, really profoundly important. This is especially important at this time.

As I think everyone knows, we have so much technological power in our hands now that we can either use to create something wonderful, or we can destroy the whole darn thing, very easily, very quickly. But to me, part of the experience of deep realization is another paradox. You are deciding to participate in life in an awake and mature way because you care tremendously and because that is your fundamental contribution to life, and simultaneously you are resting in a realization that completely frees you from the anxiety about it all.

Today, many people are very well intentioned, but they are running around with a tremendous amount of anxiety, upset, and an overt kind of rage. We also need that corresponding realization of how profoundly okay everything is to go along with the understanding of how profoundly out of balance everything is. Then, we are not acting on anxiety, we are acting on truth and Love.

LML: Without that deeper understanding that everything is okay, we can't really face how out of balance things are. That is what makes it possible to truly face it—a connection to something larger that is already totally okay. This is also what makes it possible to face our own conditioning.

Adya: Yes, I agree. Each of us has a small part to play. If each of us takes responsibility for our small part, then we don't have to worry about how big it is. What is really important is whether we are taking responsibility for our part, big or small.

The last thing I would like to say is that whether or not someone is awakened to any degree, they need to begin to seriously contemplate taking responsibility for trying to manifest the deepest thing they know, whatever that may be. Unawakened people know some very profound things, if they just care to look. They know some of the really deep values of human existence. They don't have to be awakened to really know those things. I think the people who have had some awakening, in order for them to embody it, also need to take responsibility for the deepest thing they know and begin the journey of what it is to actually live that out and be with all the challenges and do whatever work they have to do in order to live that out. I think that ultimately, whether someone is awakened or unawakened, the embodiment in one sense is the same thing. It is just taking responsibility for the deepest thing you know and beginning to act on it. It would be wonderful if everyone did nothing but that.

JLW: I'm hearing you say something else also, Adya. There is an inner compass or gravity that we all have. Everyone knows a deeper truth about what it means to be a human being among others. It is important for us to get in touch with that and honor it to the extent that we will do whatever is required to live as that.

Adya: That is really well put. That is exactly what I would have hoped to say. I do think that human beings have an instinctual sense of some very beautiful high truth and virtue. One of the myths is that you have to be really awake to be in touch with those truths. I don't think that is true. I have seen many people who are unawake, spiritually, but have extraordinary lives of deep integrity and they really are honoring the deepest thing that they know. Often, the deepest thing that they know is the deepest thing the mystic knows, or very close. It's not that far away. That is beautiful, because that means that you don't necessarily have to take a leap to begin. The leap is becoming honest about wherever you happen to be.

The longer I teach, the more I have a real respect for what we are asking people to do. It is really an immense thing. The ultimate reality is here all the time effortlessly…but to really live it, is a life's work.

That is true for everybody, awakened or unawakened. It's a real journey that takes huge commitment and it is not easy. The longer I do this, the more I develop respect for anybody who is even trying. It's really something for a human being to decide they want to live from a deep place of honesty and truth, awakened or unawakened. I have a lot of respect for people even making the effort because it is a big thing to ask.

The nice thing is that there is more and more support for this all the time, which is heartening. There are even more of our leaders who are trying to do the same thing. We need many more of these leaders, but at least there are some. And, how many people were talking about this stuff thirty to forty years ago? Not many!

I am really glad that you are working on this book and making your own contribution to it. I have always seen both of you as two of the more committed people I have known since I have been doing this work. It's been great being part of the ride with you.

LML: It has been great having you as a guide on the ride!

The Fruition of Awakened Relating

My sincere intention is that this book will contribute to creating an opening and a wider conversation about how we can relate and live more in alignment with what is most true. It is the natural expression of John's and my shared intent to awaken together and serve the whole. This book is an offering from the heart of our relationship to all beings.

We all have a contribution to make, and it doesn't matter how big or small it appears to be. Couples such as Adayashanti and Mukti are reaching many people. For others, it may be a quiet overflowing of Love that is not widely noticed. We each have a gift that we are destined to unwrap for the world, a one-of-a-kind sacred offering of Love and benefit. This natural, spontaneous movement that grows beyond the couple to serve others is what I see as the fruition of awakened relating.

Appendix
Additional Stories of Awakened Relating

Healing Relational Trauma in Awakened Presence

Lucia's Story: Releasing Fear in the Ultimate Safety

Even though Lucia had a history of sexual abuse trauma, she was not sure that she needed psychotherapy when we first met. She doubted that the abuse had any effect, however she knew she had a lot of fear. Lucia was so good at deeply burying her feelings, it seemed to her that the feelings related to the abuse, other than fear, were not even there. Lucia was so shut down, she was not able to feel much of any emotion, even positive ones.

As children, Lucia and her sisters were molested by their grandfather while he lived with them. They would take turns staying up all night to keep him out of their bedrooms, which of course did not always work. Unfortunately, her parents, who were victims of abuse themselves, were unable to protect them. Lucia first told this story without emotion and with a great deal of detachment. She had disconnected from the trauma. She later reported that her body would just shut down if any of memories or feelings related to the trauma began to emerge. Even in dreams about the abuse, she shut down any feelings related to it.

In therapy, we started to focus on the experience in the body very slowly and gently. We practiced simply feeling her body and allowing her to be seen by me while saying, "I am here." This was very difficult since she spent most of her time hiding and looking down, without making eye contact. Lucia was so anxious about being seen that she would not talk in class at school, and avoided doing anything that would bring attention to herself. This included not pursuing her artistic talents because she felt exposed when people looked at her artwork. Lucia's fear was so extreme that she was often unwilling to go out and get the mail or take out the garbage without her partner accompanying her.

Lucia became a radically different person after awakening to her true Self. She sat up straight and looked me right in the eye, maintaining contact throughout the sessions. She spontaneously began giving me hugs, which had never happened before. She was now here and fully present. Lucia was clearly no longer the frightened, meek Self she previously took herself to be. She woke up out of that identity to a remarkable degree. This usually happens more gradually and less dramatically for most people.

Lucia no longer hid from her feelings. She saw them as expressions of her true nature. It was now possible for her to be fully present with them. In her words, "I feel safe, supported, and held inside. This makes it possible to be with the emotions, thoughts, and memories of the trauma. Before knowing the presence of my true Self, I was totally blocking all of that." Lucia learned to rest in her deeper nature and allow it to hold her as she experienced feelings she had never felt before.

The greatest challenge that arose from Lucia's abuse was learning to sleep alone. She had never slept alone in her life, and never in the dark. She always had to have a light on, even when someone else was there. Throughout her young adult life, Lucia always made sure she had a partner or roommate to sleep in the same room with her. However, when she found herself living alone for the first time, she was forced to learn to sleep alone. Fortunately, Lucia was ready to face this fear.

Lucia began by sleeping alone with the light on. "At first, I was only getting a couple hours of sleep a night. I would just be with the fear and feel it, and not get carried away by it or the thoughts about it.

I just stayed present with it all. It was a reprogramming of my mind, body, and nervous system. Every time the fear came up, I could also feel the deep knowing that I'm okay. There was a deep sense of safety that allowed me to stay present with the fear. It took about three weeks to learn to sleep alone and another couple of weeks to sleep with the. light off. Now I'm okay with it all. I can sleep alone. I can sleep in the dark. There is no fear now, and there was so much fear for so long!"

This healing took place entirely by allowing all of the fear to come up in the presence of her deeper nature. Lucia did this on her own outside of therapy sessions. Even though most people need therapeutic assistance to face traumatic experience directly, Lucia's courageous process shows what is possible by relying on awakened awareness alone.

Finding Stillness in the Eye of the Storm

Phoebe's Story: Healing Relational Wounding

When Phoebe first came to therapy to work on her trauma history, she had not yet consciously recognized the awareness that is her essential nature. She had, however, been exposed to spiritual teachings that spoke of this awareness for several years. I could see it shining brightly through her eyes, but she tended to doubt that she really knew this directly. As this aware presence was repeatedly pointed out over time, Phoebe came to acknowledge what was already obvious and stopped doubting that she had a direct experience of this.

Phoebe grew up in a frightening environment that included frequent physical abuse and domestic violence. As a baby, she was also left to cry alone in her crib for long periods of time. This resulted in an insecure attachment and relational trauma, which diminished her capacity to regulate emotions and stress. All of this created a life-long history of relational and emotional instability.

In the beginning stages of treatment, I would support Phoebe in being with the waves of intensity that would arise by using skillful, therapeutic means and supportive touch. We would go into it together,

a little at a time. Phoebe had very strong surges of emotions and energetic releases, which easily overwhelmed her nascent sense of presence
without support.

As awakened awareness became more stable and present in her
experience, we would sit together with our eyes connected in a relaxed
gaze and unite in shared Being. We would then allow all the emotions,
sensations, and energies to come up and move through with as little
resistance as possible, which allowed them to release. This release was
made possible by direct experience of the vast, unifying ground of
Being while staying in relationship. Phoebe would cry or tremble and
terror or rage would arise. Rather than going into stories about it, she
dropped her attention into the body and away from her habitual labels
and descriptions, and just allowed the sensations to move through
without needing to name or analyze them. If she needed to talk about
her experience, that was allowed too.

Body-based methods for working with trauma were also applied to
support her nervous system in staying present with the powerful sensations and emotions. Even with awakened awareness, when there is
trauma, it is important to work with the nervous system to develop
resilience and the capacity to be present with what is. I know this
because it was essential in my own process to develop stability in my
nervous system, which taught me how to facilitate that for my clients.

As Phoebe met her experience directly in the presence of awareness with therapeutic support, the process would eventually settle on
its own and resolve into a deep opening of peace and stillness. At the
end of one such session she looked at me and said, "I have no idea how
I could fully release this trauma without recognition of the presence of
awareness, my true nature. I have no idea how it could be possible!"

It was important for Phoebe that I sit with her through these challenging emotions and sensations. This helped heal the insecure attachment that was created by being left alone crying in her crib as a baby.
As we gazed together in shared Being, we would often work with the
attachment issues by noticing what came up in the body around being
in relationship, while simultaneously noticing the safety of the secure

ground of Being. We would sit together in the field of awareness in relationship, while being aware of body sensations.

Phoebe was able to transfer this relational work to her relationship with her husband. She became willing to take responsibility for her reactions and learned not to project them onto him. She came to know that even if the reactions appeared to be triggered by him, they were not about him, and she was able to wait until the reaction settled before talking to him about it. Once the waves moved through, she could then say something to him about what was triggered, but only from a centered place of non-blame. As a result, her marriage was less and less negatively impacted by her relational trauma.

Practicing Awakened Relating

Simon and Isabelle's Story: Relaxing into Spaciousness While Relating

Simon and Isabelle are another couple who are using the practice of relaxing for short moments into the spaciousness of Being in their relationship. They met shortly after Simon's divorce when they traveled to India as friends to attend a spiritual event. While traveling, they both realized quickly that there was more than a friendly connection and they had a powerful experience of falling in love. Although this was very romantic and passionate for them, their experience was very different from any other time of falling in love in the past. They were able to relax into their shared Being together, something neither had experienced previously. Simon reports, "Being able to really relax together was the quality I had been looking for all my life. I had brief glimpses of this before, but now it was more like this relaxed heart-to-heart connection was the natural state of being together."

Simon and Isabelle knew from the start that they were sharing a connection to the source of Love, rather than seeing each other as the source. Simon says: "We were just bringing ourselves to a meeting in Love and not trying to get it from the other. It was clear that we both knew that Love was inherent. It is the great ground quality that we share and we can access together easily. That Love is the platform that we shared from the start. From that platform things can come up and we can trigger each other, but it seldom happens. It is all totally okay when we share that ground."

The following is a conversation I had with Isabelle and Simon about their experience with awakened relating. They began by sharing the differences in how they experienced intimate relationship before and after recognizing the common ground of Being.

Simon: In previous relationships, it was hard work to just keep my head above water. I felt like I was in a boat that was sinking and using all my energy and effort to pump the water out of the boat to keep it from sinking, but it was sinking anyway. It was exhausting. I would use affirmations to create a feeling of more self-love, and there was a lot of self-focus. I spent lots of time looking for methods to heal my former relationship. I spent so much energy and time trying to fix it from the perspective of something being broken. There was also a lot of processing and sharing about how the other person upset me, and I was doing techniques to keep from feeling invaded, and so on. I had a lot of concepts, such as believing it was important to live with an open heart, but I wasn't able to actually do that. So, there was a lot of effort and struggle to try to open the heart. I had so many concepts about how to create a feeling of closeness and intimacy.

Since recognizing my true nature and sharing this in my relationship with Isabelle, there is a feeling of being connected in a natural way, without any effort involved. The connection comes through relaxation and the feeling of openness. If Isabelle shares something, it is much easier to stay open and present without effort. I no longer get triggered so easily by her and I am more receptive. If you are not trying to protect yourself, you are much more receptive naturally. I no longer feel that I have to always protect myself, as I did in former relationships.

Isabelle: I wanted to have a healthy, love-based relationship. I came to understand that I had lost self-love and self-respect in my past relationships. So, I made a commitment to myself to never, ever make the same mistake again. I was totally ready for a relationship based in ultimate reality. I was open to finding a man who I could share this reality with, and I was okay if it did not happen. I knew I was ready for awakened Love. That was the only kind of relationship left for me. When I first met Simon, I knew he was the man I could share this with. It was obvious. The relaxation that we fell into just by being together was so compelling to me. It was so clear that meeting here, in Being, would give us a steady ground to move through the difficult parts of relationship.

I knew that it would be quite a challenge to be in relationship with Simon when we came home from our trip after being in "paradise" together. We had a complicated reality back home. Simon was newly divorced with three small children and an ex-wife who lived close by. However, I was committed to having a good relationship with his ex-wife and the children and having a harmonious new family constellation. It was helpful that we could meet in the embrace of our spiritual community. I trust in that, and it is still a challenge for me.

I don't think I could have handled this situation in the way that I have without the support of our community, and without knowing my true nature. It has made a huge difference. The situation with the three of us—Simon, his ex-wife, and myself—is similar to my childhood set-up. I come from a very shattered and unusual upbringing. I lived with my mother full-time and my father was married to another woman, who he had always been married to. The three of them had a very difficult time relating with each other. So, I already had experience with triangles in relationship. By the time I met Simon, I had a lot of clarity about what I wanted to bring into relationship and what was mine to work with within myself. This helped me to clarify my understanding of my childhood patterning and to embrace that in my heart.

I want to honor my relationship with Simon because it is such a beautiful journey to share a commitment to rest in all that comes up in relating, to just rest in Being with the other. And, to move out of self-centeredness to see that we can move together in everything that comes up in relating and that this expands us beyond ourselves. I can see that it is amazing how two people can support each other to grow together in Love and to be able to expand that Love into benefitting others. For example, our relationship is focused on benefitting the children. It is beautiful to see how they are growing and thriving in the confidence we have in our true nature. We all feel so much better in this. That is a direct result of our relating in the relaxation of Being.

LML: Please give an example of what you mean by "moving together with whatever arises in relating."

Isabelle: For example, sometimes there are misunderstandings between us. It could be my personal issues that get triggered, or the difficulties of all the details of daily life dealing with the children. These things are uncomfortable. Also, my father died recently. That was a big change for me, which put me in a life crisis. I could also see how steady Simon was from resting in the stable ground of Being, which made it possible for him to be with me through the whole process of grieving my father's death. It gave me strength to have Simon be there with his stability, which supported me in moving through that with so much more ease.

I now clearly see all my ideas about love and what love should look like. All of my concepts about love are becoming normalized. I am experiencing much more freedom within all the ideas now, not taking them to mean anything and instead experiencing the moment to moment expression of true Love, *as it is* without all the ideas and expectations. Now, relating is a spontaneous unfolding in the moment, rather than something that comes out of old ideas and concepts. It is just what it is in each moment. Love just is. Love is just here. And, each time that I recognize that it is always here, I see that awakened relating is all about recognizing what is already here.

Simon: Yes, it is beautiful to experience living with less and less agendas and concepts. In fact, the concepts are falling away. They pop up and then we relax with them and then life opens up more. It is also important to look at concepts about relating. There are so many out there. By reading so many books, I gained a lot of concepts about what a relationship should look like and how a man and a woman should be, and so on.

LML: Please share more about resting for short moments in your true nature while experiencing relationship challenges.

Simon: Sometimes short moments of resting in my nature can be very subtle and sometimes they can feel expansive. It is often the very subtle things that can be the biggest challenges in the relationship. The core reason for a problem is because I want something from the other person. It can be small things. For me, one thing that happens from time to time is when Isabelle is frustrated or emotional, I believe that I have to fix her. I think this is very common among men and women. I used to go to that place very often. First, I would think it was my fault that she was feeling frustrated and emotional, and I would feel invaded by her emotions. At the same time, I felt responsible for fixing her and returning her to harmony again. Since this was not possible, it was very frustrating for me. It has been a long journey for me to relax with the impulse to fix my partner. Still, if I pick up a slight frustration or any feeing of disharmony in Isabelle, the first impulse is to think, "What have I done wrong? Did I do something?" And normally she will say, "No, it has nothing to do with you." Then, I would still try to change how she feels. I have had to relax with that pattern a lot. It has been the deepest and most challenging pattern for me to move through. But, I have been able to relax with this, listen without reacting, and allow Isabelle to feel whatever she is feeling. I will maybe give her a hug, or offer support, but not try to take her out of her experience.

LML: These patterns can be very deep and go back to our childhood.

Simon: I can see clearly where this pattern came from. It came from taking care of my mother. For the longest time, it was automatic and unconscious. So, the first step was to become more aware of the pattern in myself, and then slowly give it some space without acting on impulse. This is challenging to do. It comes from a frightened child's fantasy that he would be totally alone and not provided for if his mother collapsed into her emotions, so he had to take care of her. It is a very deep impulse based on survival. Each time this pattern arose, I did short moments of resting as the open, clear presence that is the basis of this impulse. This practice was extremely powerful. The effect has been dramatic. These short moments of resting reconnect me with the source where everything dissolves by itself when left unrejected.

Isabelle and I had invested a lot of time and energy into different approaches, desperately searching for a way to be able to deal with our relationships with others and ourselves. Being a "seeker" can be a strong habit and identity. However, all approaches were based on the assumption that there was something wrong that needed to be fixed, released, or worked out. There was a lot of hard work needed and an imagined result projected into the future, which always kept it out of reach. From discovering our basic ground nature and practicing relaxing as that with all that comes up, we now see clearly that the satisfaction and fulfillment in life can only be found in allowing everything to be as it is in the here and now.

Acknowledgments

First and foremost, I would like to offer deep, loving gratitude to my husband John Lumiere-Wins. He went through the entire manuscript for this book with me countless times and was a consistent source of support. It was truly a joint effort. I don't think this book could have happened without him. I would also like to thank him for all the years of loving-kindness and for his commitment to practice awakened relating.

I am especially grateful to my daughter, Elizabeth Siverts, for her wise feedback and loving support, as well as for the design of my website.

I would like to acknowledge and express my gratitude to all friends and colleagues in my community who contributed to this book. I was supported by my community in so many ways, including by you sharing your stories in the book, providing encouragement and inspiration, giving feedback as readers, and providing writing retreats, editing, endorsements, and more. I would like to thank each of you individually.

I offer heartfelt gratitude to Margo King and John Steiner for your support, consultation, and generosity, and for sharing your story of awakened relating.

I acknowledge and offer loving appreciation to my dear friends Premsiri Lewin and Roberta Godbe-Tipp for your ongoing love, support, and encouragement.

I give special thanks to Marlies Cocheret, Patricia Resch, Roberta Godbe-Tipp, and Jeff Tipp for sharing your quieter homes for writing retreats.

I would like to express my deep appreciation and gratitude to each and every one of you from my spiritual community in the Bay Area and around the world who shared your stories of awakened relating in this book. Since most of you wished to remain anonymous and use pseudonyms, I will not list names, but you know who you are.

Special thanks to the nondual spiritual teachers who contributed their wisdom and stories of awakened relating: Adyashanti, Marlies Cocheret De La Morinière, Ellen Emmet, John Prendergast, Meike Schuett, Isaac Shapiro, and Rupert Spira. Also, a special thanks to tantra teacher Carla Verberk for sharing her story.

I would also like to acknowledge those who provided feedback and editing as readers: John Astin, Glenn Francis, Premsiri Lewin, Pernilla Lillarose, John Parker, John Prendergast, Shakie Roth, Judith Shiner, and Elizabeth Siverts.

I offer a heartfelt gratitude to my community of colleagues who endorsed this book. Thank you for your support.

I would like to offer a special acknowledgement and heartfelt gratitude to my clients for their courage in facing their relational wounding and willingness to share their stories in the book.

I would like to express great appreciation and gratitude to the editors who assisted me through the many years it took to complete this manuscript before it was accepted by New Harbinger: Marjorie Bair, Priya Irene Baker, Lane Keller, John Lumiere-Wins, Victoria Ritchie, and Jennifer Stewart. Your contributions were essential to the completion of this project.

I learned that it truly takes a village to write a book! Each one of your valuable contributions is sincerely appreciated. A deep bow of gratitude to you all!

References

Adyashanti. 2004. *Emptiness Dancing: Selected Dharma Talks of Adyashanti*. Los Gatos, CA: Open Gate Publishing.

Adyashanti. 1999. "The Heart of Relationship." Accessed December 2010. https://www.adyashanti.org.

Adyashanti. 2006. Satsang talk at Asilomar Retreat.

Adyashanti. 1999. Satsang talk "Relationship with Everything."

Adyashanti. 2006–2010. *True Love: The Heart of Awakened Relationship*. Louisville, CO: Sounds True.

Adyashanti. 2012. *The Way of Liberation: A Practical Guide to Spiritual Enlightenment*. San Jose, CA: Open Gate Sangha.

Adyashanti and Mukti, spiritual teachers, in discussion with the author, November 2014.

April, in discussion with the author, May 2014.

Carla Verberk, therapist and tantra teacher, in discussion with the author, August 2014.

Catherine and Michael, in discussion with the author, April 2014.

Chopra, D. 2006. *The Path to Love: Spiritual Strategies for Healing*. New York: Harmony Books.

Christiane Prendergast, singer and spiritual teacher, in discussion with the author, June 2014.

Deborah, in discussion with the author, January 2014.

Ellen Emmett, psychotherapist and facilitator of Authentic Movement, in discussion with the author, July 2014.

Fisher, H. 2005. *Why We Love: The Nature and Chemistry of Romantic Love*. New York: Owl Books.

Gendreau, G., Peyser, R., and Gentille, F. 2010. *Marriage of Sex and Spirit*. Santa Rosa, CA: Elite Books.

Hubbard, Barbara Marx. 2006. "The Suprasexual Revolution." *The Marriage of Sex and Spirit*, edited by Gerilyn Gendreau. Santa Rosa: Elite Books.

Huber, C. 1997. *Be the Person You Want to Find: Relationship and Self-Discovery*. Murphys, CA: Keep It Simple Books.

Huber, C. 2001. *There's Nothing Wrong With You*. Murphys, CA: Keep It Simple Books.

Isaac Shapiro and Meike Schutt, spiritual teachers, in discussion with the author, July 2013.

Isabelle and Simon, in discussion with the author, March 2014.

John Prendergast, psychotherapist and spiritual teacher, in discussion with the author, June 2014.

John Steiner and Margo King, nondual transpartisan consultants, in discussion with the author, October 2014.

Katie, B. 2002. "The Work of Byron Katie: Do the Work." Accessed June 2014. http://thework.com/en/do-work.

Lucia, in discussion with the author, February 2014.

Marlies Cocheret De La Morinière, tantra teacher, therapist, and spiritual teacher, in discussion with the author, September 2014.

Parnell, L. 2013. *Attachment Focused EMDR: Healing Relational Trauma*. New York: W. W. Norton & Company.

Peterson, J. 2013. *The Natural Bliss of Being*. Seattle: CreateSpace.

Phoebe, in discussion with the author, June 2014.

Richo, D. 2002. *How to Be an Adult in Relationship: The Five Keys to Mindful Loving*. Boulder, CO: Shambhala Publications.

Rupert Spira, nondual spiritual teacher, in discussion with the author, May 2014.

Sherab, K. P. R. and Dongyal, K. T. R. 2012. *Pointing Out the Nature of Mind: Dzogchen Pith Instructions of Aro Yeshe Jungne.* New York: Dharma Samudra.

Spero, D. 2015. *Easy Grace: Meditations on Love, Awakening and the Ecstatic Heart.* Sedona, AZ: David Spero Publications.

Spira, R. 2013. *Ashes of Love: Sayings on the Essence of Nonduality.* Oakland, CA: Non-Duality Press.

Steve and Tracy, in discussion with the author, July 2014.

Tanahashi, K. 2016. *The Heart Sutra: A Comprehensive Guide to the Classic of Mahayana Buddhism.* Boulder, CO: Shambhala Publications.

Tolle, E. 2005. *A New Earth: Awakening to Your Life's Purpose.* New York: Penguin Books.

Tolle, E. 1999. *The Power of Now: A Guide to Spiritual Enlightenment.* Vancouver, BC: Namaste Publishing.

Tolle, E. 2003. *Stillness Speaks.* Novato, CA: New World Library.

Urgyen, T. R. 2000. *As It Is, Volume II.* Hong Kong: Rangjung Yeshe Publications.

Watson, E. 2014. "Pornography Addiction Among Men is on the Rise." New York: Huffington Post Blog.

Welwood, J. 2006. *Perfect Love, Imperfect Relationships: Healing the Wound of the Heart.* Boston: Trumpeter Books.

World Food Programme. Accessed November 2017. http://www.wfp.org.

Lynn Marie Lumiere, MFT, is a seasoned psychotherapist with a focus on transforming issues at their source through dissolving the belief in separation that creates and sustains them. She is dedicated to awakening consciousness and meeting life's challenges as doorways to greater freedom. Her work is sourced in over forty years of dedicated spiritual and psychological exploration, as well as almost thirty years of marriage and practicing psychotherapy. This experience led her to the understanding that no matter what the problem, transformation and freedom from suffering is possible when we tap into the infinite and ever-present source of Love. She has been especially interested in applying this understanding to healing relationships and trauma.

Lynn Marie has been involved in the exploration of non-dual wisdom and psychotherapy since 1998. She is a repeat presenter at the annual Nondual Wisdom and Psychology Conference and the Science and Nonduality (SAND) Conference, and is a contributing author to *The Sacred Mirror.* Lynn Marie is also coauthor (with John Lumiere-Wins) of *The Awakening West.* Her primary spiritual teacher is Adyashanti, and she has studied with many other teachers from non-dual, Buddhist, and Hindu traditions. She lives in Grass Valley, CA.

For information about Lynn Marie and events she offers, please visit www.lynnmarielumiere.com. It is her intention to offer support for learning and experiencing awakened relating.

MORE BOOKS for the SPIRITUAL SEEKER

ISBN: 978-1684031047 | US $16.95

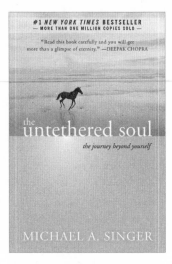

ISBN: 978-1572245372 | US $16.95

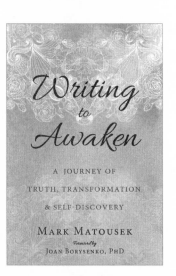

ISBN: 978-1626258686 | US $16.95

ISBN: 978-1626256415 | US $13.55

newharbingerpublications

NON-DUALITY PRESS | REVEAL PRESS

Sign up *for* our spirituality e-newsletter:

newharbinger.com/join-us